# BIG SKY GHOSTS

## EERIE TRUE TALES OF MONTANA

### Volume 1

### DEBRA D. MUNN

PRUETT PUBLISHING COMPANY
BOULDER, COLORADO

Printed in the United States
10  9  8  7  6  5  4  3

Library of Congress Cataloging-in-Publication Data

Munn, Debra D., 1953–
    Big sky ghosts : eerie true tales of Montana / Debra D. Munn.
        p.    cm.
    Includes bibliographical references and index.
    ISBN 0-87108-838-X (pbk. : alk. paper)
    1. Ghosts—Montana. 2. Haunted houses—Montana. I. Title.
BF1472.U6M849    1993
133.1'09786—dc20                                                    93-3176
                                                                         CIP

Cover design by Kathy McAffrey
Book design by Jody Chapel, Cover to Cover Design

To my parents, John and Bonnie Munn,
who have loved and encouraged me,
and who made me believe
that all things were possible.

# Contents

Acknowledgments                                                    ix
Introduction                                                        1
Who's Haunting Carroll College?                                    9
Things That Go Bump in Bannack                                    14
She's Not Gone                                                    19
Montana's Vanishing Hitchhikers                                   25
The Ghost Who Didn't Like the Rolling Stones
  (and Other Spooks at the U of M)                                33
The Skull of Bone Basin                                           40
Edith, the Ghost of the Mansion                                   42
The Sheepherder's Cane                                            47
Ghosts of the Little Bighorn Battlefield                          50
The Mystery of the House in Philipsburg                           74
"The Ghastly Form with Silent Tread"                              80
Accompanied by Angels                                             85
"Hoodoos" at the Butte–Silver Bow County Courthouse               86
Some Ghosts Are Good Guys                                        102
This Property Is Condemned!                                      107
The Gracious Lady of the Grand Street Theater                    113
Spooks Galore in Mining City Mansions                            123
Appendix: Additional Readings                                    137
Index                                                            141

# Acknowledgments

I want to thank all those whose names and stories appear in this book, as well as the newspapers and magazines that published my letters and articles asking for Montana ghost tales. I am also deeply grateful to the following people and organizations who helped me put this project together: Donna Atkins, Priscilla Baker, Jean Baucus, Bear Creek Saloon (Bearcreek), Martin and Mary Lou Behner, Pat Bick, Bureau of Land Management, Dr. Merrill Burlingame, Butte Chamber of Commerce, Butte–Silver Bow Public Archives, Art Carey, Kay Carey, Jamie Carr, Michael and Colleen Casey, Dr. Lynne Chadwick, Conrad Chamber of Commerce, Kristie Constantine, James Court, Ellen Crain, Carolyn Cunningham, Carl Darchuck, Marge David, Kitty Deernose, Helen Detwiler, C. W. Dolson, Ann Drew, Bob and Deb Enders, Paul Fees, Jane Fellows, Ralph Ferraro, Frank Fitzgerald, Andrew Fleming, Maggie Fones, Ghost Research Society, Ron Gusick, Leida Hafer, Helena Chamber of Commerce, Patrick Hill, Jim Hinkle, Chuck Hollenbaugh, Dwight Huber, Natalie Hughes, Bruce Jacobson, Joyce Jensen, Dale Kaczmarek, Jamey Karr, Jerry Keenan, Nan Kemp, Connie Kenney, John and Margo Keserich, Ken and Patti Kowalczyk, S. Lambros, Russell Lawrence, Jim Leaf, Mary Lenihan, Lewis & Clark Library, Dr. John Lohman, Lois Lonnquist, Sue Lowe-Barbosa, William Lowe, Jr., William Lowe, Sr., William and Barbara Lowe, Jean Mathews, Doug McChristian, Donna McClure, Mike McGraw, Debbie Meyers, Roy E. Millegan, Missoula Chamber of Commerce, Missoula County Library, Montana Historical Society, Montana Historical Society Library, *Montana Magazine*, Montana State Library, Judd Moore, Carol Morris, Dr. John A. Morris, Charlene Murdo, Earl Murray, Art Myers, Sandie Oller, Dr. Daniel J. O'Neill, Vivian Paladin, Charlotte Patrick, Pam Peterson, Maggie Plummer, Mary Potts, Tom Power, Bill Raoul, Tana Reinhardt, Jane Richards, Dr. Don G. Rickey, Dan Ripley, Dr. Paul S. Rosenthal,

# ACKNOWLEDGMENTS

Dr. G. James Rowling, Dr. Dennis Sacry, Joe and Peggy Sandman, Jackie Schmeltz, Mark Schultz, Bette Schutte, Dr. Edward D. Schutte, Priscilla Serafin, James Silva, Dorothea Simonson, Wally Small, Teri Sporkin, Howard R. Starkel, Ben Sterhan, Patty Sterhan, James (Putt) Thompson, Ben Tone, Rick Varady, Dave Walter, Mignon Waterman, Jan Woods, Barbara Wroe.

# Introduction

Mention the subject of ghosts and most people automatically think of eerie, creaking mansions in the East—or even more remote, of musty, drafty, and decidedly ancient castles in Europe. Few people are likely to associate a western state like Montana with either the supernatural *or* with mansions—and yet, after three years of collecting tales, I can verify that the Big Sky State has more than a respectable share of both spooks and stately homes—although Montana's spirits are often partial to less traditional kinds of haunts.

Take, for example, the phantom who plays with the elevator in the Butte–Silver Bow County Courthouse—he may be the shade of a murderer hanged over eighty-five years ago. And then there are the weird goings-on in Bannack and Garnet, where the term "ghost town" is particularly appropriate. Montana can also boast of spooks in mines, specters on battlefields, and wraiths on the road—hitchhiking, no less. And ghosts in the state's theaters are so plentiful that their dramatic escapades alone could fill a volume.

To collect these stories, I interviewed over one hundred people and searched through countless books, magazines, newspapers, and files of historical organizations. I have attempted to tell each tale as completely and accurately as possible and I have used real names as often as I could. When interviewees have preferred to be anonymous, I have given them a pseudonym. I have also used a pseudonym to protect the privacy of families of certain individuals now deceased.

Readers will notice that some names, especially those of theater folk, appear in more than one chapter. The reason may be that some people are more prone to supernatural occurrences than others or it could be that some locations, such as theaters, are more apt to absorb psychic impressions. Consider, too, that since drama people frequently travel from place to place, they have more opportunities to experience strange things at a variety of sites.

......
1

One of the most frustrating things about putting together a collection such as this is that it can never be complete. For one thing, encounters with the supernatural keep occurring, especially in certain psychic "hot spots." Paranormal phenomena are impossible to predict with any degree of certainty, but the odds are better than average that unexplained events will continue to take place at the Little Bighorn Battlefield, at Virginia City, and at Helena's Grand Street Theater, to name just a few haunted locales. And even though there are no stories set in Billings in these volumes, I'm sure that some must exist. I heard about one involving a modern house, but attempts to contact the couple living there were unsuccessful.

Another frustration is learning about an especially interesting story too late to investigate it. Just as I was about to finish the writing of these chapters, for example, I learned that Boulder Hot Springs in the south-western part of the state has been the scene of some rather dramatic occurrences involving a ghost called Simone. The story goes that Simone was a secretary who was shot and killed at the resort while she was working or vacationing with her boss.

Beth Pross is an employee at Boulder Hot Springs, which was constructed in stages from 1888 until about 1910. She has had many uncanny experiences in the old buildings, although she has never felt particularly threatened. On one occasion she heard the faint ghostly strains of big band music, perhaps a lingering echo from the resort's heyday in the 1930s and 1940s. Beth has also witnessed the transparent apparition of a woman—perhaps Simone herself—strolling around a courtyard and walking around the edge of an old pool that was destroyed by an earthquake. And once, while Beth was relaxing on the veranda, she heard some "thumping, bumping, and clattering" nearby, but whoever was causing the noise was invisible.

Beth told me that one of the owners of Boulder Hot Springs had an even more startling encounter with the ghost. This woman peered into a dresser mirror in her room on the west wing, only to find the face, hairstyle, and clothing of another woman reflected at her.

During my research, I also encountered some interesting stories that weren't detailed enough to make a chapter, but which were too good not to include somewhere. The experience of Michael Gordon in the fall of 1971 is one of these. Before he became the caretaker of Garnet, Mike was living in what had been the old general store in the nearby town of Bearmouth. Next to the old store was a large two-story white boardinghouse-hotel that had been vacant for years. At the time of Mike's experience, the hotel was jacked up and due to be moved three miles down the road.

Mike was tilling his garden one day when he looked up to see the figure of a man who appeared to be in his late teens or early twenties. "I saw him walk out the back door of the hotel and off of the porch—and then he disappeared right into the hillside," Mike insisted.

The next evening Mike had dinner with the adopted daughter of the man who had owned the store and, without letting her know that anything unusual had occurred, he asked her to describe her deceased father. She said that he had been a rather heavy man, five feet eight inches tall, and that he usually wore bib overalls and a big black denim jacket—the kind that railroaders used to wear. Mike said nothing, but he knew from her description that the apparition he had seen was that of the woman's father, wearing those same clothes. Mike also learned that there had once been a building at the exact spot where he saw the specter walk into the hillside.

It's interesting to speculate that psychic impressions may have been released when the old hotel was being jacked up to move. But no one is sure why the Historical Museum at Fort Missoula should be haunted and some of its employees don't believe that it is, in spite of a story by Evelyn King in the *Missoulian* a few years back. According to the article, doors open and close mysteriously, invisible footsteps make floorboards creak, and objects seem to move around on their own.

The current curator of collections, L. Jane Richards, believes that the occasional unexplained noises are attributable to the fact that the building is settling and that the so-called ghost is a convenient scapegoat taking the blame for human forgetfulness.

Maybe so, but Kathi Olson was curator at the time the article appeared and she insisted that tools often disappeared only to reappear in unlikely places. Although secretary and registrar Darla Bruner Wilson doesn't really believe in the ghost, she told the *Missoulian* reporter that the security alarm often clicked on and off when no one was present to activate it. She recalled also that most of the incidents had occurred during periods of remodeling.

Strangest of all was the behavior of an 1896 music box that had been loaned for an exhibition one Christmas. It had to be wound up and switched on to play and yet it came on and off by itself three different times.

A more X-rated phantom may be spending some time in the Dumas Redlight Antique Mall in Butte, according to owner Rudy Giecek. In 1982 Rudy bought what had been the last brothel in town and turned it into an antique mini-mall. The two-story red brick structure at 45 East Mercury is all that remains of a block of once-flourishing houses of ill repute built originally to provide services to miners.

"The building was a brothel from 1890 to 1982," Rudy told me, "and according to the last madam, one of her predecessors had committed suicide there in 1954. She took an overdose of pills after a married man who had promised to take her away never showed up. The poor woman had her bags packed and was waiting to go. The madam told me that, after the suicide occurred, several of the girls had seen a ghostly figure walking up and down the stairs."

Rudy claims that he's never experienced anything unusual himself, but an artist renting one of the upstairs rooms complained that she often felt a presence that interfered with her painting. "She felt that someone was actually trying to paint through her," Rudy said, "and she ended up destroying a couple of paintings because they weren't what she'd intended to create. The sense of a presence became stronger after the *Montana Standard* ran an article about the place in February 1991. Now the artist does most of her painting at home."

About a week after the story appeared, the reporter who had written it drove by the building and saw a woman painting up in the artist's studio. Deciding to stop by for a visit, the reporter parked his car and got out to ring the doorbell. He clearly saw a woman standing at the easel, pacing back and forth while he rang the buzzer, but she never came to open the door.

"When the reporter told me what had happened, I assured him that the artist never went up there at night and that I have the only keys to the building," Rudy explained. "When he heard that no one could have been there that evening, he just turned white."

A school in Brockton in northeastern Montana is apparently the home of a more innocent, although less tangible ghost. Roger Rock taught at a school on a reservation there, and he remembers hearing footsteps in the building when he was alone late at night. He repeatedly asked who was there, but he never received an answer. Eventually, he learned that the building was supposedly haunted by the spirit of a schoolboy who had been run over by a train. Roger doesn't recall whether the boy's death was suicide or an accident.

Another young person who apparently died tragically forms the basis for an eerie tale set near a youth camp at Legendary Lodge on Salmon Lake near the Bob Marshall Wilderness Area. "A girl named Mary evidently fell off her horse and was killed near there," explained Bill Hunthausen, who has worked at the camp since the 1960s. "The horse returned home, but the girl never did and no one ever found her body. I know that this part of the story is true, and it may have happened as early as the 1940s.

"A wooden grave marker inscribed with Mary's name was erected in the mountains," Bill continued, "and the story is that it moves from place to place, although it never strays far from the same general area. From week to week, it will be found in a different spot, often a couple hundred feet from where it was before. I've actually seen the grave marker in different spots myself."

A lovely legend from Fort Benton concerns the ghost of a dog named Shep who is Montana's version of the Scottish Greyfriars Bobby. "Shep's master died and the dog watched as the man's body was placed in a casket and loaded onto a train," explained Stacey Gordon. "The story is that every day after that, Shep would go to meet the train, thinking that his master would return to him. There's even a monument to the dog in Fort Benton on the hill and people still report seeing his apparition from time to time."

The following two stories also involve protective, watchful spirits, but I was unable to confirm anything about them. The first appeared in *Phantom Encounters*, a volume in Time-Life Books' Mysteries of the Unknown series (Alexandria, Va.: 1988, 65). No names or dates are given, but the story involves a Butte dentist who was saved in the nick of time from administering novocaine to a patient.

Just as the dentist was about to inject the shot, the phantom of his deceased mother appeared, warning her son that the man was allergic to novocaine and wanted to die in the dentist's chair. That way, the ghost explained, his death would be blamed on the dentist and the patient's family could collect his life insurance.

The doctor then asked the patient why he had not mentioned his allergy to novocaine and the man admitted that after a previous injection he had blacked out. Three doctors had spent several hours bringing him back to consciousness.

The extensive bibliography in the Time-Life series does not indicate where individual stories come from, so I wrote to the editors at Time-Life to find the source. I received no answer, so my next step was to send a letter to every dentist and dental supplier listed in the Butte area telephone directory. I received eight replies, all to the effect that no one had heard this story.

The second tale concerns a guardian spirit and was told to me by a man who heard it firsthand many years ago. In the summer of 1969, a hotel in a Montana city was ablaze and two firefighters were called to the scene. A violent explosion occurred, disorienting the men; one of them looked up to see the figure of a phantom firefighter motioning the way out. The apparition looked like a turn-of-the-century fireman, complete with a long handlebar mustache. The men followed his directions and made their way safely out of the building.

Both of the firefighters who were saved by the guardian spirit are now deceased themselves, so I wrote to their widows to ask what they knew about the story. I also contacted the fire chief in the same city and he told me that no one he had talked to had ever heard the tale and, moreover, that the widows of the two men were very upset by my letters.

For this reason, I will not reveal even the city where this incident reportedly took place, but I don't understand why anyone would be upset by such an uplifting, comforting tale. I can't say the same for the next story, however, which turned out to involve something other than poltergeists at work.

Nine mysterious fires in eight days occurred in January 1958 at a home in Glendive. Firefighters were called repeatedly to the house at all hours of the day and night and by the end of the ordeal over three thousand dollars' worth of damage had been done. Family members lost most of their clothing and several of them suffered burns on their hands and injuries from smoke inhalation. The *Daily Ranger* kept readers informed about the blazes but, even though investigations were conducted after each one, no cause was discovered. After the ninth incident, a story appeared in the paper with the announcement that the fire chief promised to give a full report of the affair at the next meeting of the City Council. As far as I could tell, however, there were no more stories regarding the subject.

At the suggestion of Tana Reinhardt, the managing editor of the *Ranger-Review*, I wrote to Montana Fire Marshall Jim Leaf to ask for the solution to the mystery. His response was that all the fires had been set by a troubled fourteen-year-old granddaughter living in the house with her mother, sister, grandparents, and aunt. The girl's father was in the military, stationed in England, and the teenager had set the fires because she was angry at being left behind to finish the school year in the United States.

Because she was a juvenile, the girl's name was not divulged and no public report was given to the City Council. A short time afterward, the teenaged arsonist got her wish to go to England and fires no longer plagued the house.

As this example shows, some "ghost" stories turn out to be something else entirely, but there are still plenty of unexplained occurrences to keep lovers of the supernatural happy—so many, in fact, that it was necessary to divide these Montana tales into two volumes, the second to be released at a later date.

While there is no way I can guarantee that the stories in these books are "true" in any way that can be proven, I believe in the sincerity of all the people I interviewed. The final judgment about the eerie phenomena will have to be made by you, the reader. So—what are you waiting for?

# One

# Who's Haunting Carroll College?

C ollege students are generally fascinated by the supernatural, so it's a rare institution of higher education that doesn't have at least one ghost story making the rounds, whether it has any factual basis or not. Carroll College in Helena, Montana, has had more than its share of spooky phenomena over the years, experienced by students, faculty, and staff alike, and at least some of these happenings seem connected to events in the school's past.

Many of the weird occurrences have taken place in St. Charles Hall, where a blocked-off fourth-floor bathroom with mysterious bloodlike stains on the sink has generated all kinds of rumors. A tragedy did occur there about thirty years ago, but many of the students at Carroll College, as well as a number of faculty and staff, have never heard the truth about it.

Matthew Kelly (a pseudonym) was a student at the college in the early 1960s. Well liked and fun-loving, Matt returned to the dorm late one night after partying in Helena. He had probably had too much to drink and when he was in the bathroom that is now blocked off, he somehow fell and hit his head, causing a severe cerebral hemorrhage, from which he died.

David Miller, now a high school teacher in Helena, knew Matt when they were both students at Carroll College. "He wasn't a close friend of mine, but I played football with him, and he was a really nice guy," David said. "His death was a terrible thing and it shocked and saddened all of us that a young person with so much promise could die in such a senseless way.

"The ghost stories connected with him didn't start up until I'd already graduated from Carroll, although sometimes students reported someone knocking on their doors when no one was there. And shortly after Matt's death there were rumors that the bloodstains where he fell in the bathroom couldn't be removed. The maintenance people would scrub them, but they kept coming back."

Rumors about the bloodstains are still rife on campus. According to Margaret Hoagland, who worked in the maintenance department from

1983 to 1991, the first thing incoming freshmen want to see is the bathroom with the bloodstains, and the fact that the area has been blocked off only adds to the mystique. Twelve or thirteen years ago, Pete Ruzevich was a student who also worked for the maintenance department at Carroll and he remembers what a big deal it was to be allowed to see the bloodstains.

"At first the head of maintenance didn't want to show the bathroom to us new guys, but we kept hearing about it and were curious," Pete said. "We kept asking the other maintenance people to take us up there and finally they did, but only after they'd really built up our expectations.

"I finally saw what everybody had been talking about and it looked like regular dried blood, all right. It was splattered all over a sink and I thought it strange that no one had cleaned it up. I'd heard that the stains had been there for years and that someone had committed suicide in the bathroom. If it isn't blood on that sink, then somebody did a very convincing job of making it look real."

And that, according to Margaret Hoagland, is exactly what happened. Not long after Matt's tragic accident, some pranksters used red paint on the sink and that's why the "bloodstains" could never be washed off. Margaret doesn't believe the stories that the stains were removed, only to reappear, and she claimed that the reason the bathroom itself was later blocked off was because it became outdated and too expensive to renovate. Now, Margaret explained, the room is used only for storage.

Although she doesn't believe the gossip about the bathroom, Margaret does admit that strange things happen at Carroll College. She remembers hearing that a female cafeteria worker saw a ghost one Sunday morning when she was waiting to serve breakfast to the priests. "It was in the summer and she was sitting there having coffee when she saw an apparition," Margaret said. "Nobody could tell her who it might have been, but the woman was sure of what she saw. And apparently, before this happened, she had never heard any of the stories about the college being haunted."

Margaret herself had only one eerie experience while she was working at the school. "Two students from St. Charles Hall were killed in a car crash in Elliston and for about a week afterward the building felt like a morgue," she recalled. "When I first walked into the dorm the day following the accident, the feeling was very oppressive. You didn't have to see anyone or talk to anyone—you could just tell that something terrible had occurred."

Most of the ghost stories around Carroll College involve other tragic events that have supposedly taken place over the years, although, unlike the well-documented death of Matthew Kelly, these are not easily verifiable. One story is that someone killed himself by jumping from a window, or as former student Aaron Haggins has heard, from the top floor in the north stairwell of St. Charles Hall.

"The windows have been boarded up to prevent anyone else from jumping, but people say that you can still see and hear the guy falling," Aaron explained. "There was also supposed to be another young man who fell down some stairs between floors and the story is that you can hear wailing on the stairwell in that area."

Most people believe that the person who threw himself to his death was a student, although current student Debra Dacar heard that he was a priest. She may be confusing the story of the suicide with that of a priest who reportedly fell, hit his head, and died in St. Albert's Hall. Another possibility is that this latter story is confused with the circumstances of Matt Kelly's death, since the details are so similar.

One story that is clearer and more plausible is that during the 1930s a young nun became ill and died on the top floor of St. Albert's Hall. Ed Noonan, former director of St. Charles Hall from 1986 to 1990, is familiar with tales regarding the phantom sister. "Students sometimes sense that she's with them, or they catch glimpses of her, but I've never experienced those things myself."

Former student Kathryn O'Connell wonders whether the entity who sometimes visited her friend's room in St. Albert's might not have been the ghostly nun. "We never saw a figure and she didn't come every night, but her visits always occurred at the same time," Kathryn said. "Sometimes my friend and I would sit on the bed and wait for her. We could hear footsteps coming down the hall and, although the door to the room never opened, the handle turned. Then we heard footsteps across the wooden floor and we felt the presence of someone standing at the window. After a few minutes, we heard her going back to the door and walking down the hall again. Even though we didn't actually see an apparition, we always sensed that the presence was female."

St. Albert's Hall is now the Student Union, but the ghostly nun still walks the halls and Aaron Haggins has heard her. "It was about two in the morning and I was helping a young lady close the place up," he remembered. "Just the two of us were there and we had already made sure that the doors upstairs were locked. We were standing in the kitchen at the far end of the building when we heard someone walking on the floor above us. My friend went up there to check again, but she didn't find anyone. We started closing up the kitchen and again we heard someone walking upstairs. As we began heading toward the door, the footsteps seemed to move with us on the floor overhead and when we stopped, they stopped. When we finally got to the door, we heard the footsteps walking back in the other direction. We finished locking up and got out of there as fast as we could."

Students and staff have reported other unearthly beings at the college, such as the invisible priest who strolls down hallways tapping his cane and an unseen presence who sits on beds. This bed-sitting spook also seemed to prefer easy listening to rock music, since it changed the radio dial whenever its human companion left the room.

Another female student awoke one night to the sound of her best friend's voice calling her. "Julie, Julie," the voice repeated from the hallway. When Julie went to see what her friend wanted, she saw that the hallway was deserted; she learned later that her friend had no knowledge of the incident.

Probably the most unaccountable occurrence of recent times is what happened to Debra Dacar when she lived in St. Charles Hall. "Lots of girls experienced all kinds of freaky things there and I encountered a ghost myself in one of the bathrooms," she said. "It was exactly midnight and I was sitting in one of the stalls when I heard the outer door of the bathroom swing open. I didn't hear any footsteps following that, but I looked down so that I could see under the stall and I heard the door of the one next to me opening. I could feel the presence of someone there, but I could plainly see that whoever it was didn't have feet or any other visible body parts. When the toilet in there flushed, that's when I jumped off the one I was on and got out of that bathroom. I never believed in ghosts before I came to Carroll College, but I definitely do now."

As irksome and even alarming as the spooks may be, they don't always play the role of troublemakers. Ed Noonan recalls sensing a presence in St. Charles Hall whenever a student living there had a serious problem. "It was almost as if an unseen someone were watching out for the well-being of students," he explained. "One girl told me that when she was very sick with the flu, she felt someone in her room keeping her company, even though her door was locked so that no one could come in. She wasn't at all frightened, but rather comforted by the presence."

Aaron Haggins believes that the entire college is protected by someone and, as proof, he points to a train wreck that occurred near the campus a few years ago. "The brakes gave way and the train rolled backwards for miles before derailing just as it got to Carroll College," he recalled. "The buildings themselves received substantial damage, with lots of windows blown out all over campus. There were also problems caused by severe cold because the temperature that day was way below zero. But not a single person was seriously injured and as far as I'm concerned that was a miracle."

While many people associated with Carroll College agree with Aaron that unseen presences abide there, not everyone is a believer. One administrator even told me that in his opinion, the terms "true" and "ghost story" were mutually exclusive and that all accounts of psychic phenomena at the school were a lot of bunk. That's a practical, no-nonsense assessment and it sounds logical during daylight hours. But students in the dorms and other buildings know that at night, when the halls finally quiet down, the ghostly priest will come tapping with his cane and the phantom nun will make her rounds to comfort the sick.

# TWO

# Things That Go Bump in Bannack

I f having more than its fair share of shoot-'em-ups and hangings is
what causes a place to be haunted, then Bannack, first capital of the
newly created Montana Territory, should be fairly crawling with
spooks. This typical Wild West gold mining town was, after all, the head-
quarters for outlaw sheriff Henry Plummer and his robber gang, the Road
Agents, and it was also the place where many of them, including Plummer
himself, were rounded up by a secret group called the Vigilantes and
brought to justice on the gallows.

With so much robbing and killing in Bannack's past, we might reason-
ably expect to hear that Plummer's spirit takes occasional midnight strolls
up Hangman's Gulch or that the shades of gunfighters frequently reenact
their battles to the death inside Skinner's Saloon. Well, perhaps they do;
though, to my knowledge, no one has seen them. For, oddly enough,
in this real-life "ghost town" that knew so much well-publicized violence,
almost all of it by men upon other men, the only ghosts I've been able
to dig up have been those of women, children, and animals.

Lee Graves, a descendant of one of Bannack's founding families and
himself a photographer and author of the delightful *Bannack: Cradle of
Montana* (Helena, Mont.: American & World Geographic Publishing,
1991), admits that in a ghost town, tourists often come looking for spooky
stories and if they don't actually find them, they imagine them.

"But there are a couple of tales that really do seem to have something to them," Lee said. "Several times, visitors have reported hearing
a baby crying on the southeast side of town, in one of the old cabins
that used to belong to early resident Amede Bessette. People ask whether
anyone with small kids could be living there now. Of course, no one
does, but the story is that either eight or fourteen babies died there of
various diseases, including colic, typhoid fever, and smallpox. Epidemics
of all kinds were quite common in the old days and many of the graves
in the cemetery are for children who died in the mid- to late 1880s. There
are also quite a few from around 1913."

Visitors to Bannack have reported hearing the ghostly sounds of babies crying in the cabin on the left, which once belonged to early resident Amede Bessette. (*Photograph courtesy Lee Graves*)

The ghostly crying is mentioned in a Halloween 1989 article by John Barrows of the *Dillon Tribune*. In "The Ghosts of Bannack," Barrows wonders whether the babies are still crying in memory of that long-ago sickness and death. Perhaps a more likely explanation for the eerie sounds, if they really exist, is that the babies' suffering was of such intensity that it somehow psychically imprinted the noise of their crying onto the walls or floors of the old cabin, to be "played back" under the right conditions.

A more classic Bannack ghost story involves Lee Graves' godmother Bertie Mathews who died several years ago at the age of ninety-three. "When she was a young girl, her best friend was a gal named Dorothy Dunn, and those two kids were as close as they could be," Lee explained. "One summer day Bertie and Dorothy were together in one of those big swimming holes in Grasshopper Creek. I don't recall how it happened, but somehow, Dorothy drowned. Her death really bothered Bertie and she went through many hard times because of it.

"Sometime later, when Bertie was in her mid-teens, she was walking in the upper story of the old Meade Hotel, which her mother managed at various times through the years. Suddenly, she saw an apparition of her beloved friend. Dorothy was wearing a long blue gown, and her hair was flowing.

"This incident scared Bertie so much that she hardly ever talked about it," Lee said. "When I was a kid, my dad and I used to visit her quite often and, although he repeatedly asked her to tell us the ghost story from the hotel, she always refused. She would try to laugh it off and change the subject. But her older sister Georgia finally told Dad what Bertie had seen. All I know is that if Bertie said it happened, it did. She wasn't superstitious at all, and she was quite religious."

Other stories about the Meade Hotel involve dogs that refuse to go inside. One of these dogs belonged to Dr. Dale Tash, the present curator of Bannack and professor of history at Western Montana College at Dillon. While Dr. Tash firmly rejects the idea that phantoms exist, at Bannack or anywhere else, he did admit that his dog was frightened, and of an entity much more horrifying than a mere specter—a skunk!

If they are indeed true, two final legends about Bannack appear to have all the right ingredients for ghost stories, but strangely enough, I found none in connection with them. In spook lore from around the world, one of the surest ways to stir up spirits is to bury someone improperly or to disturb that person's final resting place. When Henry Plummer and two of his Road Agents were hanged in the wintertime, on January 10, 1864, the ground was frozen hard and the gravediggers didn't feel like going out of their way to bury what they regarded as lowlife scum. Therefore, the bodies of Plummer and the two men hanged with him, as well as that of another Road Agent hanged previously, were all buried fairly close to the surface.

According to Lee Graves, a few years afterward a doctor who was interested in Plummer got very drunk one night and dug up one of the outlaw's arms. "No one is sure who the grave robber was, but he may have been Dr. Glick, the same physician who had taken care of Plummer years before when he'd been shot in the elbow," Lee explained. "But whoever the man was, he was extremely inebriated and because he was on his way to a dance he thought he'd better get rid of his grisly find. So he left Plummer's arm, still covered with flesh, in a snowbank outside the dance hall.

"The doctor then went inside to enjoy himself, but he got a big surprise about thirty minutes later. His dog had been digging around in the snowbank, latched onto Plummer's arm, and carried it right into the dance hall to savor it in warmth and comfort. You can imagine how fast that broke up the party."

Bannack's abandoned Meade Hotel, where Bertie Mathews once saw the apparition of her friend, Dorothy Dunn, who had drowned several years before. (*Photograph courtesy Lee Graves*)

In his book on Bannack, Lee Graves tells two versions of another local legend about the fate of Henry Plummer's remains. The first and most probable says that around the turn of the century two drunks dug up Plummer's skull and deposited it on the back bar of Bannack's Bank Exchange Saloon. There the curious relic reposed until the saloon burned and, with it, all its contents. The second story is undoubtedly just that, a story, but is nevertheless fascinating. This account relates that the same old drunks dug up the skull, which finally found its way into the hands of a Bannack doctor. The unnamed doctor sent the specimen "back east to a scientific institution for study to try to figure out why Plummer was so evil."

If this second version has any truth at all, no one knows just what conclusions were supposedly drawn about Henry Plummer's nasty character. But it does seem a bit odd that Bannack isn't swarming with the ghosts of Plummer and his Road Agents. Could it be that they had enough of terrorizing their fellow citizens while they were alive?

If the outlaws ever do decide to return, they will still be able to recognize their old stomping grounds. True, over the years fires have taken their toll on some buildings, others have simply deteriorated and fallen down, and some structures have been moved (in the case of the Goodrich Hotel, all the way to Virginia City, about eighty-five miles away). Other buildings were torn down for their lumber or even for firewood, but Plummer-era landmarks such as the Crisman Store, the Carrhart House, and the Xavier Renois House are still standing. It is the goal of the Montana Department of Fish, Wildlife and Parks to preserve rather than to restore Bannack, so that this little mining town will never be the flashy, overly commercialized tourist trap that some other historical places have become. Instead, Bannack will always be a ghost town in the truest sense of the word.

# Three
·········

# She's Not Gone

Does the human personality survive the death of the body, and do spirits return to earth to comfort and assist the loved ones left behind? Over the past four years, Dorothy Johnson and her family have had more than their share of sorrow, but out of their troubles has come a strengthened conviction that dying does not mark the end of our existence.

On June 6, 1988, the Johnsons' beautiful, blonde, twenty-one-year-old daughter Mary lost her battle with cancer. Like all parents who lose a child, the Johnsons were devastated. But a series of events since then has convinced them that Mary is still a vital part of their lives.

In the fall of 1987, Mary was in her junior year at Montana State University in Bozeman. She was majoring in nursing, and she was in love with her boyfriend, Duane Mattfeldt. At first, she attributed her overwhelming fatigue to the stresses of college life, but when the pains in her abdomen didn't go away, she called a doctor and was scheduled to undergo a complete physical examination.

A short while before the checkup was to take place, Mary drove back home to Hinsdale to visit her family and to watch her sister Linda play in the district basketball tournament. During this trip, she suffered excruciating pain and when she returned to Bozeman she decided to see the doctor right away.

On November 25, 1987, Mary was found to have an advanced case of colon and ovarian cancer. She immediately began chemotherapy treatments in Billings, but her condition kept getting worse.

In spite of her illness, Mary tried hard to make her life as normal as possible; the one thing she wanted more than anything was to marry Duane. They had been going together for several months and on April 16, 1988, they were married in a church wedding in Malta, Montana. Afterward, the young couple tried to settle into their new home, but Mary kept losing strength. She was also undergoing weekly blood tests and spending more and more time in the hospital in Glasgow, thirty miles east of Hinsdale.

······

By the end of May, Mary was suffering from an accumulation of tumor fluids and moved into the hospital on a permanent basis. Duane and his mother-in-law Dorothy kept a constant watch at her bedside, but there was little they could do except offer their love and support.

Dorothy believes that her daughter had an uncannily accurate idea of just how long she had to live. "When Mary was moved into what would be her last room," Dorothy remembered, "she looked around at the wallpaper and said, 'Well, this is really nice. I could stay here two weeks.' As it turned out, she was in that room exactly fourteen and a half days before she died."

Just three or four days before the end came, Mary did something else that would become eerily significant some time after her death.

"I was sitting with her when she slowly raised her right arm and pointed to a corner of the ceiling," Dorothy recalled. "She had been sleeping and the sudden movement surprised me. I asked her, 'What do you see, Mary?' And she answered, 'My car.' Well, Mary owned a 1985 red Ford Tempo that had been a gift from her grandmother and my husband and me. I couldn't figure out why she would think of it at a time like this, so I said, 'Your car? Are you going someplace?' Mary wrinkled her brow, shook her head, and said, 'I don't know.'"

Mary died on June 6 and on June 10, the night before her funeral, Dorothy and Duane were in Glasgow taking care of last-minute business. Mary's father, brother, and sister were all riding in the same red Ford Tempo, headed for a service at the mortuary in Glasgow. Suddenly, the car quit running.

Luckily, the family members weren't stranded for long, since they were able to borrow a neighbor's car to complete their journey. The Ford Tempo still wouldn't start the next day, however, so the Johnsons had to drive their pickup to the funeral. It wasn't until the fuel pump was repaired a week later that Mary's car began running again.

About three weeks later, on July 15, Dorothy was driving the Tempo to Glasgow. She had an appointment at the beauty parlor and she also planned to take Mary's wedding dress to the cleaners before having it preserved in a sealed box.

"As I drove up to the crossroad leading to the cemetery, I suddenly had this compelling urge to visit Mary's grave," Dorothy explained. "I looked at my watch and realized I had plenty of time, so I drove right up to the grave site and stopped the car.

"As soon as I opened the door, a huge cloud of black smoke billowed out from under the hood on the driver's side. I grabbed my purse and dashed around to the back door to rescue Mary's wedding dress and some other clothes. Then I ran as fast as my legs would carry me," Dorothy said. "My arms were full and I was so frightened that I kept stumbling. It seemed that with every step I took, I dropped something and had to pick it up—all the way across the cemetery. I was scared to death—what if the gas tank blew up or the burning car started a grass fire?

"I screamed and screamed for help, but nobody heard me," Dorothy explained. "When I got far enough away, I looked back to see the car completely engulfed in flames. Especially eerie was the way the fire illuminated the headlights, making them look as if somebody had turned them on. They looked just like a couple of eyes watching me.

"The car never did explode, but within ten minutes it had completely burned up—right beside Mary's grave. As I staggered over toward the road, two pickups arrived from town, driven by men from the grain elevator. Fortunately, they had seen the fire when they left work to go to lunch. A fire engine and an ambulance showed up a few minutes later and the medical technician drove me to a friend's house to examine me. My blood pressure and pulse were a little high and my throat burned from the smoke, but otherwise I was unscathed."

Dorothy's daughter Linda soon arrived to take her to the emergency room in Glasgow, where she was given oxygen to flush the smoke from her lungs. "Linda said that as she was coming to get me, a little dust devil crossed right in front of her," Dorothy recalled. "She got goose bumps up and down her spine and the thought running through her mind was 'There goes Mary!'

"I really believe that Mary's spirit saved my life that day," Dorothy insisted. "If I had been on the highway when the car started to smoke, there's no way I could have gotten myself out in time, especially since I'm a rather large woman. The car burned so fast that I would hardly have had time to unfasten my seatbelt. And the strangest thing was that I'd never had the slightest intention of visiting Mary's grave that day, until I got right to the turnoff to the cemetery. Mary was definitely my guardian angel."

No definite cause for the fire was ever established, although the fuel pump that had malfunctioned earlier was ruled out, since in Ford Tempos it is located in the rear, rather than the front. And it wasn't until some time after her frightening experience that Dorothy connected the fire with Mary's pointing at the ceiling and talking about the car.

"Another thing that crossed my mind was that right after Mary died, there had been some family discussion about who should own her vehicle," Dorothy remembered. "Mary wouldn't have liked any quibbling, since she had always been the peacemaker. But after the fire, there was no longer any car to argue about, so the issue was settled once and for all."

Dorothy admits that the experience with the fire is the spookiest thing that has ever happened to her, but her daughter Linda believes that she and her roommate may actually have seen Mary's apparition.

"Just a few months after my sister died, I was a student at Northwest College in Powell, Wyoming," Linda explained. "Around two o'clock one morning, my roommate Connie and I were talking to another friend in our room at Cody Hall. This girl, Erica, had lost her mother several years before and the experience had been so painful that she still didn't like to discuss it. I told her that talking about Mary actually made me feel better.

"Eventually, Erica went back to her own room and Connie and I decided to go watch a movie. On our way downstairs, I happened to look out of a window that faced onto the parking lot. I could clearly see my pickup, but I couldn't believe what I saw inside.

"You see, whenever Mary sat in a car or truck, she always put her arm along the back of the seat. And inside my pickup, I saw what looked like a person sitting in exactly that position. I asked Connie if she saw what I did and she agreed that someone appeared to be sitting there. We may have been fooled by a trick of light or shadow, but it did seem strange that we had just been talking about Mary when this happened."

The Johnsons felt Mary's presence again when her father Keith was diagnosed as having liver cancer only a year after his daughter's death. Doctors didn't have much hope that he would survive one particularly critical surgery, but on the night before it was scheduled Linda dreamed about Mary. In the dream, the two sisters were sitting across a table from each other, giggling and acting silly as they had done many times in real life. Linda interpreted the dream as a message from Mary that their father would survive the operation and, as Dorothy said, "He came out of it with flying colors."

On the day I called Dorothy to check out some final details before writing this chapter, she said, "It's odd that you should call today, because of what happened a little while ago. My car was stopped at a light and another car made a turn in front of me. I could have sworn that the girl driving it was Mary. Her hair was the same color and the same style, exactly. I saw her for just a second. And then you called."

Dorothy believes that her daughter may have had premonitions from a young age about her death. "I remember when she went to visit my father who was dying of cancer in 1980," she said. "Mary turned very pale when she saw him, as if she were frightened, and I've often wondered if somehow she knew that she would face the same illness. And after she died, we found a poem she had written to a boyfriend sometime between 1985 and 1987. Part of it reads, 'Who knows where my journeys / will lead me / for I have many destinations / in my short life time!'"

Two days before Mary died, Dorothy herself felt a compulsion

Mary Johnson Mattfeldt on her wedding day, April 16, 1988. (©*1988 by Farrell Studio, courtesy Dorothy Johnson*)

to write an essay that was later read at the funeral. Dorothy believes that her writing that day was inspired by something or someone outside herself. "I got the idea for it when Mary's friend Valerie was visiting her in the hospital," Dorothy recalled. "I watched them together, remembering that they had talked on the phone a lot during their school days. Then I began to wonder how friends and family could communicate with Mary after she died and suddenly all these words just came to me."

Dorothy entitled the essay "She's Not Gone," and it perfectly describes the close relationship that everyone in the family still has with Mary, a relationship that, if anything, has become stronger since her death. With Dorothy's kind permission, portions are excerpted below:

> You'll know she's answering you every time you hear the whispering of the leaves in the trees, the rustling of the grasses in the pasture, the lapping of the waves on the water, the light pattering of raindrops on the garden, the sighing of the breezes on the hillsides, and the chirping of the birds on a bright summer morn.
>
> There can be no doubt in your mind that Mary is with you when you see her eyes twinkling at you from the stars in the skies, her friendly

wave in the swaying of the grain in the field, the blush of her face on the petals of the rose, the encouraging pat of the wind on your back, and her smile, her lovely smile, on the face of the bright, full moon.

Mary is not gone: she's with us, keeping in touch with each of us in her very special loving, caring way, always and forever.

So—please keep in touch!

# Four
·······

## Montana's Vanishing Hitchhikers

One of the most common themes in ghost lore around the world is that of the vanishing hitchhiker. Usually, the stories involve a young woman in distress who asks a passing motorist, most often a man, to take her home. The man complies with the request, only to discover at some point in the journey that his passenger has disappeared. In other versions, the hitchhiker stays in the car for the entire ride home, and leaves behind a personal possession which the driver attempts to return the next day. There are many variants and elaborations of this same basic folktale, but in nearly all of them the driver finds out sooner or later that his mysterious passenger was actually a phantom reappearing on the anniversary of her death, or sometimes on her birthday.

Several stories of vanishing hitchhikers have reportedly surfaced in Montana, many with very specific details that should have been easy to verify. But try as I might to find even one person who had firsthand knowledge of such an experience, I was unsuccessful. My frustrating search led me to conclude that people who pick up these ghostly hitchhikers tend to disappear right along with their passengers.

One story circulating in the Helena area closely matches the classic form of the folktale and high school teacher David Miller enjoys sharing it with students in his mythology class. "I've heard that both a banker returning from a trip to Missoula and a priest living here in Helena gave the vanishing hitchhiker rides at different times and the details of both accounts are essentially the same," he said. "In each story, the driver of the car is coming down McDonald Pass, a treacherous road that is quite narrow, when he sees a young girl coming out of a phone booth in a pull-off at the side of the road. The girl flags him down or gets his attention in some other way and the driver pulls over to see what she wants.

"The poor girl is sobbing hysterically and over and over she repeats only one thing: 'I have to get home. I have to get home. My father is worried about me; I have to get home.' The driver tells her not to worry, that he'll take her home if she tells him where she lives. She gives him an

······

address on Breckenridge, an actual street in Helena, and then she crawls into a corner of the back seat and remains there, sobbing all the way. The driver, of course, is quite concerned about his passenger, but she won't talk except to repeat that she has to go home. He drives into town and takes her to the address she has specified, where he lets her out.

"Only after the driver has dropped the girl off does he notice that she has left her sweater in the back seat of his car," David continued. "He decides to wait until the next day to return it.

"When he does take the sweater back to the house on Breckenridge, he explains to the man answering the door why he has returned. At this point, the man in the house asks why a stranger is playing such a cruel joke—the girl he's referring to was the man's daughter and she died years ago in an accident on McDonald Pass. The day on which the driver claimed to pick her up is either the anniversary of her death or her birthday, depending on who tells the story.

"That pull-off on McDonald Pass is still there," David explained, "and a phone booth still marks the spot, although it's probably a replacement of the one in the story. When I heard this tale, all the details were very specific to the Helena area, including the address where the girl supposedly lived."

David went on to say that in the late 1940s or early 1950s, an article on Helena's own vanishing hitchhiker appeared in the local newspaper, as well as in *Reader's Digest*. Therefore, my first step in trying to verify the story was to locate the articles. It was impossible to find the one in the newspaper without knowing the exact date of publication, but I searched through volumes of *The Reader's Guide to Periodical Literature* to learn that a story about a ghostly hitchhiker did appear in *Reader's Digest* in March 1955 (66: 113–15). The only problem was that this tale was not set in Helena, but in the hills and valleys of the Ramapo River in New York.

I contacted David again and he agreed that this must have been the article he was thinking of, even though it was set in another state. But Carl Carmer's story, "The Girl Named Lavender," has so many similarities to its counterpart in Helena that David's confusion is understandable. In this account, a beautiful but poor girl is given charity in the form of a castoff lavender evening dress, which she wears constantly in all kinds of weather. Around 1939 the lovely girl in the lavender dress is found frozen to death and no more is heard of her for another ten years.

Two college boys driving to a dance see a beautiful girl dressed in lavender waiting by the side of the road. They stop to give her a lift and she asks if they're going to a square dance not far away. They explain that they're going to another dance somewhere else and they ask her to accompany them. She agrees, and at the dance she tells everyone to call her "Lavender," because she always wears that color.

On the way home after the dance she feels chilly, so one of the boys gives her his coat. They take her to the rundown shack that she gives as her address and she hurries inside. Only later does the boy who loaned her his coat realize that she has taken it with her.

The next day he returns to the shack, where he discovers that "Lavender" has been dead for ten years. In a state of shock, he leaves the house and drives to the cemetery, where he finds his coat neatly folded on top of the girl's grave (the story originally appeared in *Dark Trees to the Wind, A Cycle of York State Years*, William Sloane Associates, 1949).

A similar version of this story featuring different characters was published in the December 1959 issue of *Popular Science* (175: 127–28). "The Durable Tale of Hattie the Hitchhiker" by Louis C. Jones also has a New York setting, although in a different part of the state. It is a rainy, cold night when the driver, a salesman identified as Phil Carter, picks up a lonely-looking girl by the side of the road. The hitchhiker in this account lives at a specific address in Albany and she gives her name as Hattie Fairchild. She is shivering, so the driver loans her his overcoat, which he also forgets to retrieve from her.

When he returns to the house the next day to fetch his coat, he meets Hattie's mother, who isn't surprised by his story at all. She explains to him that the day before marked the three-year anniversary of Hattie's death in an automobile accident and that her ghost had also tried to come home the year before.

The driver is disturbed by the story and goes straight to Hattie's grave, where, true to this version of the classic folktale, he finds his overcoat draped over the tombstone.

In the same article, Jones points out that probably no ghost story has been repeated so often, especially in America, and that he himself first heard it as a young man. The hitchhiker tale even predates the age of automobiles, Jones claims, for it was told originally about a young man riding a horse to a dance. On the way he met a girl and took her up onto the saddle with him, only to have her disappear before they reached her home.

Jones then explains that to a folklorist, "part of the interest lies in the fact that this is so often told as a true but unbelievable happening. It is not told the way a 'big lie' is told, but as a real experience of real people."

Another reason for the story's appeal, Jones says, is that it is always told as though it were a local happening. "[I]t was a particular road, a certain address, and it was told to the teller by someone whose first cousin knew the man to whom it happened. Try to pin down the facts and you turn from one dead end to another."

My own experience in trying to verify these stories proves Jones correct. If the Helena hitchhiker was elusive, I knew better than to try to pin down the slippery lady who disappears regularly on Montana 28 between Niarada and Elmo in the valley extending from Flathead Lake to the Little Bitterroot watershed. In a *Montana Magazine* article, "Spooky Niarada: Where things go 'bump' in the night," author Maggie Plummer claims that this female hitchhiker often disappears just as drivers stop to pick her up in the area known as "The Big Draw" (September/October 1987, 78–79). Lorrie Meeks lives in Niarada, and she knows of one instance in which a driver picked up the woman, talked to her while lighting a cigarette, looked around, and found her gone. And, in keeping with what Louis C. Jones said about these stories usually happening to a "friend of a friend," this experience is said to have happened to a relative of one of Lorrie's husband's students.

A completely different type of "appearing and then disappearing" hitchhiker was said to frequent the flat wheat country between Conrad and Valier in the northwest part of the state. David Miller taught near that area for eleven years and he served as the football coach in Fort Benton. Many times he heard the story of a male ghost who was said to appear in the back seats of cars and talk to the drivers. "I've had this verified by a lot of people—in fact, one of the kids this happened to is a friend of mine who played football in Conrad. Apparently the ghost is a teenaged boy who says he's lonely and cold and he wants to talk. But when the driver pulls the car over, the boy disappears.

"The ghost was said to be that of a Conrad high school student who had a girlfriend in Valier," David explained. "One evening after football practice he jumped in the car to go visit her. He headed north out of Conrad and turned left when he reached the narrow country road leading to Valier. Before he got into town, he had a flat tire and tried to pull the car off to the side as best he could, but it was a narrow road with practically no shoulder. He got out and began changing the tire of the rear wheel on the driver's side.

"By this time it was dusk," David continued, "and a farmer driving a truck came along and failed to see the boy beside the road. The truck ran into the boy and he was killed.

"The story was that the boy's ghost was trapped in that spot for years afterward and people who drove the road at night would periodically find him popping up in their back seats, wanting to talk. Everybody around there knew the story and they all talked about it as something that actually happened."

Since moving to Helena, David has lost track of many of the people he knew in the Conrad area, but he gave me the name of one man who claimed to have encountered the ghost. As I should have expected from my previous experience in tracking down witnesses of vanishing hitchhikers, I was unable to locate this man. There was a person in Conrad with the same name, but he didn't know the story, David Miller, or even that another man with his name had ever lived in Conrad.

Feeling as if I'd slipped into the twilight zone, I called David, and he was perplexed too, wondering if he had remembered the man's name correctly. My next step was to contact the appropriately named Carol DeBoo at the Conrad Chamber of Commerce to find out whether she or anyone in the area had ever heard the story.

She hadn't, and even after asking around a local coffee shop, she was unable to find anyone else who had. In fact, no one could even remember an accident such as the one in which the boy was said to have been killed.

"However," Carol told me, "the house where my daughter lives, just half a mile off the road between Conrad and Valier, has a ghost in it. My daughter hasn't seen it, but her roommate has, so maybe the hitch-hiking ghost got tired of life on the road and moved in."

Just as I'd lost hope of ever finding a single witness to a vanishing hitchhiker incident, I got lucky. I was talking to A. J. Kalanick about another story when he mentioned in passing that he had once run over the ghost of a hitchhiker near Black Horse Lake outside of Great Falls.

"There's quite a legend about this ghost and many people have reported running over him," A.J. explained. "My experience occurred in 1973 when I was on my way back to Fort Benton from Great Falls. I remember driving along and suddenly seeing a moderately tall man with a stocky build, wearing bib overalls and standing spread-eagled in the middle of the road. He appeared so quickly that there was no way I could avoid running into him. I hit the brakes, stopped the car, and got out, but there was no trace of another human being anywhere around. And there were no dents in my car, either."

A.J.'s mother, Hilda Kalanick, had the same experience more recently, except that she never saw whoever or whatever it was she ran over. "It was 4:30 in the morning and I was on my way to catch a plane," she explained. "I was going across Black Horse Lake as a semi was coming toward me with its bright lights on. The driver didn't dim them as he got closer, so I was concentrating on driving straight ahead.

"All of a sudden, I felt the car hit something. Whatever it was was big too, at least as large as a fencepost, because my car actually moved up, then down, as it rolled over something. Another vehicle was following very close behind me, no more than a car length away, so I couldn't stop quickly. I expected that car to run over what I had hit too, because there wasn't time for anyone or anything to move out of the way, even if it were able. But, oddly, the car behind me just moved smoothly over the road as if nothing were there.

"I was very confused by that, but I was still bothered about what had happened," Hilda admitted. "There were no signs of damage to my car, but the first thing I did after I got back from my trip was to check through the newspapers to make sure that nobody had been found dead on the highway.

"My birthday was a couple days after I returned home," Hilda continued, "and four or five ladies got together to give me a luncheon. I was telling them about my experience and one of them asked, 'Where did you say that happened?' I told her it was on the Great Falls side of Black Horse Lake.

"She looked at me and said, 'You're kidding! The same thing happened to me.'"

This woman is Sadie Lippert and her literal run-in with the legendary ghost of Black Horse Lake occurred nineteen years ago. "There were five people in our car and we were driving about 55 miles per hour across Black Horse Lake right out of Great Falls," she said. "It was about 10:30 P.M., and suddenly, out of nowhere, we all saw an Indian man on our windshield, his hands braced on the window and his mouth open, as if he were yelling for help. He had long black hair and a red scarf tied around his head over his bangs; he was wearing a blue jean jacket.

"We heard no sound, no thump, no nothing—we just saw him on the hood of our car," she explained. "We were all speechless for a second; then we all started talking at once about what we had seen.

"Five of our friends were traveling in the car behind us, and the same thing happened to them, too. The driver was a doctor, so he stopped and got out, but found no trace of anyone near the road. He called out that he was a doctor and could help anyone who'd been hit, but no one came forward. And neither car had any traces of blood or anything else to indicate that we'd run over anyone. But I can see that man on the hood of the car yet and that's why I never drive alone at night near Black Horse Lake."

While these stories aren't quite the same as the previously discussed vanishing hitchhiker tales, they at least seem to be related, and for some reason, as other researchers have discovered, people who have experienced this type of eerie incident are not so difficult to find. As with the classic vanishing hitchhiker story, there are reports from all over the world of mysterious figures who appear without warning in the middle of the road and then disappear after being struck by a car.

Any discussion of Montana's vanishing hitchhikers would be incomplete without mentioning what is certainly a legend without (we hope) any basis in reality. In his "Old One-Eye and Other Lost Souls," which appeared in the May/June 1985 issue of *Montana Magazine*, C. W. Dolson tells the story of a "man who strode the highways in a black suit and white shirt, the man with sharp and glaring eyes and a voice which makes shivers run up your spine."

The story is that on a silvery moonlit night a man driving down an empty road suddenly notices "this tall and thin feller wearing a black suit and maybe a raincoat trying to thumb a ride."

The driver stops the car and the hitchhiker climbs inside, dressed to the nines in a starched shirt, a red vest, a black necktie, and "those shiny, black, pointed-toed shoes folks sometimes wear to funerals."

The odd passenger refuses to engage in small talk, but tells the driver that his sole purpose for being there is to "check the boundaries of my claim, to know what is mine before returning to my place of business and the routines of banishment, of exile."

The hitchhiker commands the driver to stop at one point on the lonesome road and he gets out of the car, walks away, and disappears. Shortly thereafter, the driver hears the shrill, crazy sounds of horrible laughter and screams with "all the pain and misery of lost souls." And then the hideous figure himself returns, "running and leaping in fifty or hundred foot bounds . . . surrounded by red and yellow flames!"

The flashing light reveals that the pointy-toed shoes are gone and the creature's feet are cloven hooves. If there were ever a mystery to his identity before, there is none now.

And while most ghostly hitchhikers aren't as frightening to encounter as Old Nick himself, meeting up with them is bound to be disconcerting. But as we have seen in Montana and elsewhere, this sort of thing happens all the time. It was even the basis for the popular song "Laurie (Strange Things Happen)," sung by Dickie Lee in the summer of 1965. Reports of vanishing hitchhikers may be a common phenomenon worldwide, but judging from the way witnesses to the stories tend to disappear, my advice is this: If you see spectral folks thumbing for rides, you'd better run over them, or you might vanish too.

# Five
......

## The Ghost Who Didn't Like the Rolling Stones (and Other Spooks at the U of M)

**M**ost hauntings take place in a fairly limited locale—a particular room, a specific hallway, or a certain floor of a multistoried structure. But the University of Montana in Missoula has no fewer than four haunted buildings and the spooks inside don't restrict their supernatural shenanigans to any special areas—they seem to enjoy wreaking havoc throughout.

Take the old theater in the Fine Arts building, for example. Here a spiteful phantom plays tricks on people such as Mary Vollmer Morrow, a student at the university from 1973 to 1977. Years later, Mary still gets the creeps when she thinks of the time she was teased by the ghost.

"A group of us were leaving for a Montana Repertory Theater tour and we were supposed to meet early in the morning at the Fine Arts building," she explained. "I arrived before anyone else, around five o'clock, and even though I hated being alone in that place, I went inside. I kept wishing the others would show up and, finally, I heard the outside door open. Then I felt a draft, just as if someone had come in.

"Glad that somebody was there to keep me company, I ran to see who it was. But when I got to the door, I found it still locked with no sign that anyone had come through it. I stood there puzzled, and I heard the opening and shutting of the other door where I had just been waiting and felt another draft. I ran back again, but no one was there either, and that door was still locked too. This sequence of events happened four or five times, making me so uncomfortable that I decided to wait outside."

Mary also recalls that faculty members often brought their children to rehearsals and on more than one occasion the kids looked down from the balcony where they were playing and saw a mysterious person sitting in the audience. "None of us on stage could see him, but the children insisted he was there," she said.

The strangest occurrences from Mary's days at the university came

......

during a production of *Macbeth*, always considered the "unlucky" play by theater folk. "The night of the dress rehearsal, the entire set, including a specially built staircase, collapsed," she remembered. "And on opening night, during the scene when Duncan and his army come in, our fog machine wouldn't turn off, so the entire auditorium filled with fog. The actors couldn't see the set or each other and kept falling off the stage and the audience couldn't see the actors.

"I played one of the three witches in that play, and as we stood over our boiling cauldrons and called out names of demons, we heard horrible screams coming from the back of the theater. We asked other people about them later, but apparently no one else had heard them. I don't know whether or not the ghost was responsible for all these things, but we found out firsthand that *Macbeth* really is the unlucky play."

Mary added that no one knew for sure whose spirit was haunting the theater, but most people believed it to be that of a worker reportedly killed during construction of the building.

Whoever the entity may be, other people have also reported feeling his presence. The drama department's production coordinator, Steve Wing, felt an eerie sensation in one of the hallways of the old Fine Arts building. "I was working alone late one night in 1977 or 1978," he explained. "My office is up on the second floor and I was leaving it to go down to the theater. As I walked into this one narrow hallway with a door at each end, I just sensed that someone was there with me. I can't explain it any better than that, but the feeling was so oppressive that I put on my coat and left."

Brantly Hall is another haunted building on the University of Montana campus and the ghost there is supposed to be that of a student who committed suicide. Rumors such as this one are often hard to verify and different versions of the suicide story exist. One is that the student killed herself in the basement, while another is that she threw herself out a window. The most bizarre version of all is the one that former student Stacey Gordon heard, that the suicide victim was a young woman who stabbed herself with a metal comb after her father lost money in the stock market crash of 1929. "I went to the university for a year," Stacey said, "and I remember hearing that her dog, a German shepherd, was also supposed to be haunting Brantly Hall."

No one I talked to reported any phantom dogs, but custodian Daniel Boone has definitely experienced eerie feelings in the old hall. "Rumor has it that the student who killed herself lived on the second floor when

Brantly was still a dorm," he explained. "It was later turned into an administrative office building and, because of the extensive remodeling, it's now hard to pinpoint where the suicide was supposed to have occurred."

"I used to be a custodial crew chief in that building and I got chills every time I walked down the hallway," Daniel admitted. "One time in 1987 another guy and I were alone in Brantly Hall when it was all locked up. As we were walking through the building, we both got the same tingling up and down our spines and, on the third floor, we kept hearing a noise like someone clapping his hands together. The sound seemed to be coming out of the ceiling and it was very loud.

"We finished making the rounds of the third floor and when we came back to the stairwell where we had been earlier, a yellow slicker raincoat was lying there. We knew it hadn't been there just a few minutes before and we were certain that we were the only people in the building. And, all the while, we kept hearing that loud, inexplicable clapping sound, which gave us a prickly feeling on the backs of our necks. The noise finally became so unbearable that we left and, ever since, I've been leery of going back."

Whether or not the suicide rumors at Brantly Hall have any basis in fact, they tend to make people nervous. Drama professor Rolly Meinholtz recalls the time that one of his students, a young man from Korea, was rehearsing for an outdoor theater production. In one scene, he seemed to be hanging himself from a tree outside Brantly Hall. Campus police became so alarmed at what they feared to be history repeating itself that they rushed to his aid. Needless to say, the student was stunned at having his rehearsal interrupted so dramatically.

Another haunted location on the University of Montana campus is Jeannette Rankin Hall, named for the state's first woman senator. This building began as the university's library, but later became the law school. Now it is used mainly for classrooms. Custodian Jack Mondloch has heard doors closing when he knew that no one else was in the building and his boss, Jeanne Tallmadge, had an even stranger experience in the summer of 1981.

"A large crew doing extra cleaning was on campus and another man and I were in charge of it," she said. "He and I got together each night in Rankin Hall to discuss the next day's work and at that time we also cleaned the top floor, which consists of four classrooms.

"Generally in the summertime the buildings are only lightly used, but on one particular night we heard the sound of subdued voices coming through the closed door of the northeast classroom. It sounded as if fifteen to twenty-five people were in there carrying on a conversation, but we couldn't distinguish any of the words.

"We figured it was a class or discussion group, so we kept waiting right outside the door for it to be over," Jeanne explained. "It got later and later and at eleven-fifteen I decided it was time for those people to get out.

"I opened the door to tell them to leave—and there was not a single soul in that room. Not one person. I ran to the windows and looked out, thinking that maybe the voices of people outside had carried so that they sounded as if they were in the classroom. But no one was there, either.

"I was completely baffled by this experience," Jeanne confessed, "but when I told other people about it, they claimed to have experienced the same thing."

Just a few nights after hearing the "phantom class," Jeanne had another weird experience involving Rankin Hall. "I was walking away from the building when something made me turn around and look back," she said. "All the lights were blazing in those second floor classrooms, even though I'd just turned them off. I went back upstairs and switched the lights off again, but by the time I got outside they had come back on. At that point, I decided they could just stay that way, because I was *not* going to enter that building again.

"The same thing happened over and over that summer and one night I was with another person on the second floor when the hall light began to dim as if it were being controlled by a dimmer switch. Finally, it went off completely. Electricians took the lights apart to check them, but they couldn't figure out why they went on and off like that.

"Nobody really knows who or what is haunting Rankin Hall," Jeanne explained, "but since it used to be the law building, we like to joke that the ghost is somebody who never got over failing the bar exam."

Fellow custodial worker Bob Williams has noticed that the odd phenomena in Rankin Hall tend to occur most frequently from August through October, during a full moon. Bob's first unusual experience there occurred one August night in 1984 or 1985. "I heard noises downstairs and decided to check them out," he told me. "As I went to go down the stairs, the light in the stairwell went off. I thought someone was playing around, so I went up the stairs and turned the light back on. I started to go back down and off it went again. I walked up and turned the light on one more time and I kept my eyes on the switch in the lower section to see who was playing a joke on me.

"As I was going down the stairwell, the light went off again, but I could tell that no one had flipped the switch. So I went back up and turned it on one more time and started down the stairs. Sure enough, the light went off again. This time I just kept walking and the light continued to turn itself on and off, on and off. I'd had enough, so I left to have a cigarette."

Bob explained that for a while he wondered whether a certain co-worker hadn't somehow played a trick on him. "But then I found out that he had been way off in a different building at the time," he said. "Again, we had electricians check for wiring problems, but they found nothing that could explain the strange behavior of the lights."

Bob's eeriest occurrence at Rankin Hall took place on another late evening after the building had been locked up. "I was working in a little computer room off the main staircase when I heard a noise upstairs," he said. "I went to the second floor, but found nothing out of the ordinary except some chairs in disarray. I straightened them up and went back to the first floor to resume cleaning, when I clearly heard someone walking around upstairs. This time I stepped outside the building and hollered up at the second floor, but no one responded.

"I went back inside and I clearly heard footsteps coming down the stairs—but no one was there," Bob insisted. "I continued to hear them walking right in front of me and, as they did so, I felt a cool breeze and smelled a dank, musty odor. And then the footsteps went on into the basement. As you can imagine, I finished cleaning very quickly and got out."

Bob Williams has also encountered unexplained phenomena in University Hall, which contains administrative offices. Also referred to as Main Hall, this building has probably been the setting for more weird goings-on than any other on campus. "When we got ready to leave, we often heard doors slamming shut throughout the entire building," Bob remembered. "At first we thought a prankster was to blame, but it happened so often that people were becoming afraid to work there.

"One time we set a trap to catch the culprit," Bob continued. "We went through the building, shutting and locking all the doors, and we stationed people near all the exits. With everyone and everything ready, we waited, and sure enough, the slamming started again.

"Several guys rushed to check the doors and what they found was startling. Some doors that we had locked were unlocked; some were open and some were closed and we didn't find anyone who could have interfered with them. The door slamming continued the whole time I worked nights, and it was most frequent between 11:00 P.M. and 1:00 A.M. It's probably still going on and nobody has ever been able to explain it."

Daniel Boone has also heard the doors slam when he knew that no one else was in the building. "And these doors are solid wood, about two inches thick, with deadbolt locks on them," he explained. "Even air blowing through drafty windows wouldn't be enough to move doors that heavy. Lights also come on by themselves and we all joke about wanting to get the second and third floors cleaned before sundown, because nobody likes to be up there after dark. I'm a rational, sensible person, but I admit that several times I've been scared to death in Main Hall."

Daniel's fellow custodian Jack Mondloch said he never believed in ghosts before he started working at the university, but one night in Main Hall he heard phantom footsteps descending a staircase—when he happened to be standing at the bottom of it. Jack claims that he wasn't frightened, but merely surprised by this eerie encounter. However, another experience made him believe that the spooks were trying their best to intimidate him.

"One night I was cleaning the sinks in the men's room in the basement of Main Hall," he explained. "I was six or eight feet from the door and I heard someone knocking. I said, 'It's open,' but no one came in. I heard another knock, so I went over and opened the door myself and was surprised to find no one there. Now, this building has long, creaky, wooden hallways, and you can hear every move that anyone makes. And I opened up that door so fast that there was no time for any trickster to get away.

"I didn't want to put up with any more invisible people knocking at the door, so the next night I propped it open with a wedge," Jack said. "I was working at the other end of the bathroom, when—boom! The wedge came flying through the air and hit me in the leg. I looked all over the place for whoever had thrown it, but there was nobody anywhere near me. I felt irritated by this little episode—it was as if somebody were telling me, 'Take that!'"

Fellow custodian Jim Dredger laughed when he heard Jack's story, but one night he discovered for himself that Main Hall was haunted. "I was downstairs in the women's restroom around 1:00 A.M., filling up the soap dispensers, when I heard a knock at the door," Jim said. "I put the soap down and yelled, 'Come on in; I'll be out in two or three minutes.' There was no answer, and then I heard another knock. I walked over to the door, opened it up, and found no one there.

"I thought this was peculiar, but I figured that my supervisor or one of my friends was giving me a bad time, so I didn't think too much about it. But just to be on the safe side, I stuck a wedge under the door to keep it open. That way, if I heard someone walk by, I could look out and see who it was. I turned back around to pick up the soap canister and there in the mirror of the vanity was the reflection of a lady with dark hair.

"I was startled and I whirled around to see what she wanted, but there was no sign of her. I rushed into the hall, but I couldn't see or hear anyone moving along that wooden floor. I felt very strange, and I hesitated to tell anyone what had happened because I'd made so much fun of everyone else's ghost stories."

No one seems to have any idea who the entity haunting the building might be, but at least one custodian learned something about the phantom's taste in music.

"When I worked in Main Hall, I often took my Walkman stereo with external speakers," explained MaryJane West. "Normally, I used headphones, but the building was so creepy that I wanted to be able to hear what was going on around me. I played all kinds of music from country to experimental rock and I soon learned that every time I played the Rolling Stones or the Clash, the tape player would shut off. It didn't matter whether I was sitting right next to it or across the room—it would shut off whenever I played tapes of those two groups.

"The first few times I thought there was something wrong with the tapes. But when I played them at home, or even in buildings other than Main Hall, they worked fine. And even in Main Hall I could listen to them as long as I wore my headphones. I guess the ghost didn't mind my listening to the Stones or the Clash, as long as it wasn't subjected to them too."

The phantom music critic and the other unearthly beings at the University of Montana give new meaning to the term "school spirit," as they've certainly done their part to make campus life more interesting. With four haunted buildings and many reports of unexplained phenomena in each one, this university surely deserves a number-one ranking as a setting for the supernatural.

# Six

## The Skull of Bone Basin

Seventy-odd years ago, an old storyteller with a big handlebar mustache spun a tale so eerie that it still sends shivers down the spine of Theodore Bisch.

When he was a small child, Theodore lived ten miles south of Whitehall in southwestern Montana. During those quiet, peaceful times before radio and TV, neighbors often depended on each other for hospitality as well as entertainment. "After dark," Theodore remembers, "whenever folks heard the jingling sound of trace chains from horses and wagons rumbling by the house, they would go out with a lighted lantern and invite the travelers to come inside for coffee or even to stay all night."

In those days when neighborliness was the rule rather than the exception, some homesteaders made a chilling find in nearby Bone Basin. Six hundred head of cattle had been snowed-in there and starved to death, giving the area its name; and the appellation became even more fitting the day a human skull with a round hole in it was discovered and exhumed from the bank of a skid trail, the path over which logs were hauled out by horses.

A man whose name Theodore has long since forgotten took the skull to his home. The man's wife refused to let him keep it in the house so he took it out to the shed. Shortly afterward, the couple heard the familiar nocturnal sounds of trace chains jingling, horses clop-clopping, and wagons rattling outside.

As he was accustomed to do, the husband responded by getting up, dressing, lighting his lantern, and going out to welcome whatever neighbors were passing by. But he was greeted only by the lonely blackness of the night and no wagon in sight. Puzzled, the would-be host went back inside and returned to his bed.

Each night for a week the same thing happened. The sound of trace chains jingling, horses clop-clopping, and wagons rattling by could be clearly heard by everyone inside the house. But when the husband went outside to check, there was nothing there.

The wife began to suspect she knew the cause of the mysterious sounds. She insisted that her husband remove the skull from the shed and bury it deep in the earth, somewhere far enough away from the skid trail that it would never be uncovered again.

The husband did as his wife wished, burying the skull among many of the cattle bones of Bone Basin. That night he was relieved not to hear the phantom jingling of trace chains, the clop-clopping of horses, and the rattling of wagons passing by. The spirit belonging to the skull must have been satisfied at last because, once the grisly thing had been securely reburied, no one ever heard those sounds again.

Theodore Bisch has lived in the Whitehall area his entire life and he is now well into his late seventies. But he admits that he still gets an eerie feeling whenever he remembers the mustached man telling him and his father the story. And whenever he passes by the spot of the skull's reburial, he shivers as he remembers his father's words: "That's where the fellow sleeps."

# Seven

## Edith, the Ghost of the Mansion

*The Mansion Restaurant was destroyed by fire the night of June 11, 1992, after this chapter was written.*

With or without a ghost, few buildings in Montana have as fascinating a history as the Missoula structure now known simply as the Mansion. Built in the 1890s by A. J. Gibson, the architect who designed the Missoula County Courthouse, the lovely four-story edifice was originally the home of Thomas and Tennie Epperson Greenough and their six children. Thomas Greenough made his fortune in lumber, mining, and banking in several western states and, after his death in 1911, his widow and children continued to live in the house until ownership eventually passed on to daughter Ruth and her husband, A. J. Mosby.

This much-loved Missoula landmark on the banks of Rattlesnake Creek was undisturbed until 1964, but then the construction of Interstate 90 threatened to destroy it. The highway was planned to go right through the property, so A. J. Mosby donated the house to the community for use as a historical museum, asking that the city pay the costs of moving it to a new location. When city officials ruled out the move as too expensive, Mosby paid for it himself and decided to make the Greenough Mansion a restaurant and clubhouse for his Leisure Highlands Golf Course, located in the hills south of the downtown area.

Transporting a four-story building that weighs 287 tons is no simple task, as everyone involved in the undertaking soon discovered. Catlow Movers of Spokane, Washington, used six 100-ton jacks to hoist the structure up onto a 90-wheel trailer. With three trucks pulling and two bulldozers pushing the load, it crossed some railroad tracks and was then set down beside the Clark Fork River at the old Van Buren Street bridge.

Mosby and the movers then faced an almost insurmountable problem: how to get the house to its intended location across the river and up into the hills. The state ruled that the structure was too heavy to travel on any existing bridge and the cost of building a new temporary one just to transport a single building was too high. As a result, the Greenough Mansion was stranded beside the Clark Fork for nearly sixteen months and during this time vandals set it ablaze.

Much of the interior in the front part of the house was damaged, including three stained glass panes that had to be broken to provide access for firefighters. Mosby was undaunted by this setback and soon afterward he had a brainstorm. He contracted another firm to remove the roof and to cut the house into three vertical sections. Each of the sections was therefore made light enough to be carried across the city's largest bridge on Madison Street and the removal of the roof saved the expense of relocating power lines that would have been in the way. In July 1966, trucks carrying the three sections and the roof groaned their way up the steep incline to the new location and the house was lowered into place piece by piece. The total cost of the move came to fifty thousand dollars.

The next step was to refurbish the old house and to turn it into the restaurant and clubhouse that A. J. Mosby had envisioned. The new establishment opened for business in October 1968 and since then the Mansion has had several owners and managers, as well as quite a few incidents of ghostly activity attributed to Edith, one of the daughters of Thomas and Tennie Greenough.

"Employees claim that they set the tables with the glasses right side up, only to return to find them upside down," said Daniel Johnson, the current general manager. "And my favorite story is about a customer who heard someone weeping in the ladies' bathroom. She looked around to see whether she could be of any help, but no one else was there. She went to tell the bartender what had happened and that's when she learned about Edith. She became so intrigued that she went to the library to do research on the Greenough family and she discovered that the day she heard the weeping marked the thirtieth anniversary of Edith's death."

Daniel Johnson himself had an "Edith" experience in November or December of 1991. "It was late at night and although people were still in the restaurant, I was alone in my office," he recalled. "As I was working, I heard, almost subconsciously at first, a low plaintive wailing. I dismissed it as something happening outside, but the noise continued. I heard it clearly and then I looked up and said almost laughingly, 'Edith!'—and the sound stopped. I never did figure out what it was."

Missoula's Mansion Restaurant as it appeared before the fire that destroyed it on June 11, 1992. (*Photograph courtesy Daniel Johnson*)

Former general manager Paula Sheridan, who left in 1989 after working at the Mansion for eleven years, has probably had more strange experiences with the ghost than anyone else. "My first one occurred in October 1976 when I'd been working at the restaurant for only a short time," Paula remembered. "I was sitting in the upstairs bar telling this friend about all the weird things Edith was supposed to have done and my friend told me how crazy I was to believe in spooks. He was drinking from a big Mai Tai tulip glass at the time and he said, 'Edith, if you're out there, let me know.'

"Immediately after saying that, he reached out for the glass and it exploded right in his hands. The whole glass just disintegrated, driving one shard into his palm. I'll never forget the way his eyes opened wide when that happened. He ended up having to wear a bandage. As far as I know, that's the only mean thing Edith has ever done, but my friend clearly provoked her."

Paula's next encounter with the ghost took place on a slow night later that same year. "The bartender and I were talking and he was sitting against the bar," she continued. "All of a sudden, two rows of glasses behind him all fell off the shelf. The first row fell on top of the second row, but the glass itself didn't break. And then the huge, heavy double front door flew open for no reason. We both looked at each other in amazement. It was like having a wind suddenly blow through the room and then stop.

"After that, we seemed to go a long time without anything happening except that some employees experienced lights turning themselves on when no one was there," Paula said. "Once it happened to me, when I had been working at the Mansion about seven years. The cocktail waitress and I had left the building and looked back to see lights on in the women's bathroom. We just looked at each other, because we knew we had turned them off."

Paula also used to hear her name being whispered when she was in the restaurant by herself. "Since I was the manager, I was usually there from nine o'clock in the morning until all hours of the night," she explained. "There was this one area in the dining room where I'd walk in from the foyer and hear my name being called.

"Another time about six years ago I was sitting in the same foyer reading the paper and waiting for some Saturday morning deliveries," Paula remembered. "On the couch with me was my dog, a chihuahua-dachshund mix. All of a sudden, the dog looked up and started growling. I looked up too and saw the chandelier swinging, making a four-foot sweeping motion through the air. I knew we weren't having an earthquake because I hadn't felt any tremors. Anyway, if an earthquake had been causing the chandelier to swing, all the glasses on the bar would have been rattling too. That experience really scared me, so I got up and left the place."

Fritzie Yonce, A. J. Mosby's former secretary, was at one time in charge of the Mansion and she remembers a cocktail waitress who came running in terror out of the women's bathroom. "The toilet was the old-fashioned type with a chain that you pulled down to flush," she explained, "and while the waitress was sitting on the toilet, it flushed by itself. We told her that the ghost of Leo, one of the Greenough brothers, had done it, but of course we were just kidding her. She was really scared and she never went back upstairs after that."

Eerie occurrences at the Mansion are by no means limited to the restaurant's employees, as Dave Holy of Ace Refrigeration found out. He was repairing something at the Mansion once, when he got what he described as a "creepy, crawly" feeling for no apparent reason. "I'm sure I had that sensation just because it was an old house with lots of atmosphere, but I admit that I wouldn't want to spend the night there," he said with a laugh.

Even customers are not immune to the strange goings-on at the Mansion, as Tim Gordon discovered when he was having dinner there with his wife Stacey on Valentine's Day in 1990. Antique light fixtures, each with a single bulb, illuminated the tables and the one over the Gordons' table kept turning itself off.

"The first time it happened, we told the waitress that the bulb had gone out and she came over and hit the switch and the light came back on," Tim said. "It happened again and the waitress made a joke of it, saying that Edith had turned off the light."

The Gordons knew the manager of the restaurant, so that same evening they stayed after hours for drinks in the basement bar, which opens up onto the golf course. "At one point I went upstairs to the bathroom on the third floor and when I walked by what the employees jokingly call 'the Edith room,' I slammed the door," Tim explained. "It was dark in there and I was half scared; as soon as I got to the bathroom door, the stereo on that floor came on full blast. It was pretty scary, because no one was up there except me."

While practically everyone attributes mysterious phenomena at the Mansion to the ghost of Edith Greenough, no one can explain why it is she, rather than another member of her family, who is haunting the place. When A. J. Mosby died, Fritzie Yonce took over the guardianship of A. J.'s wife, Ruth Greenough Mosby, who had become incompetent during her later years. From Ruth, Fritzie learned more about the Greenoughs.

They were apparently a happy and devout family of Christian Scientists. Ruth and her sister Edith traveled extensively in Germany and throughout Europe and Fritzie recalls that Edith even married a German count. Although she's forgotten the details, Fritzie remembers hearing that most of the six children of Thomas and Tennie died tragically of accidents or illness and, according to their religious beliefs, without medical attention. Fritzie believes it very likely that Edith died in the house, but she has no explanation for why she is apparently still there, at least in spirit.

Is it possible that she remains simply because she loves her home and would rather be there than anywhere else? Fritzie Yonce knows what it's like to fall under the spell of the Mansion and she admitted, "The house gets to be an obsession, because it's such a grand old building." Who could blame Edith if, even after death, she feels the same way?

# Eight

## The Sheepherder's Cane

**M**oving from one house to another is stressful even when all goes well, but when folks discover they're sharing their new home with a malicious spirit, the strain can be almost unbearable. In May 1987, Tamara and Jim Fuller (not their real names) and their two young sons Chayce and Travis moved into a 1930s-era log house in the northwest part of Miles City, Montana. They were looking forward to settling down peacefully in their new residence, but strange things began happening even before they could unpack their belongings.

"From the day we moved in, everybody in the family would often hear what sounded like someone in heavy boots jogging up the stairs," Tamara remembered. "And we hadn't been here more than two months when something even more frightening happened. It was about eleven o'clock one night and I was upstairs in our bedroom. We had just turned the lights out when I saw this old man with very long hair and a beard. He didn't look like anyone I had ever seen before and he seemed to be wearing leather. I've never seen him since then and as far as I know no one else has either."

Tamara believes that a possible clue to the apparition's identity was an old sheepherder's cane found in one of the bedrooms. "We took it out of there to hang it in the living room and that was when all our bad luck seemed to begin," she said.

"First, Jim shattered his leg and fractured his skull in a woodcutting accident and he was laid up for over a year and a half, unable to work. The only good thing was that the doctor was able to save his leg. Next, three of our animals died, two of them mysteriously. Our doberman suddenly became ill and within a few weeks he could no longer control his bladder or bowels. He just dwindled away to skin and bones and we had to put him to sleep. Then one of our cats got run over and another one developed the same strange illness that the dog had had. This one also had fits of terror and would run up and down the stairs yowling, with his hair standing on end. He got to the point where he was attacking people, so we had to put him to sleep too. We never knew what was wrong with him, but it wasn't rabies or distemper.

"After all this happened," Tamara continued, "a guy who had grown up in the house across the street told us that none of the families who had ever lived in our place had been able to keep an animal alive and healthy."

Other disturbances have continued to baffle the family. Once after Jim went off to work and Tamara had just gotten out of the shower, the smoke detector in the hallway went off for no apparent reason.

"I climbed up on a chair to pull the cover off and stop the loud noise, but I didn't know how these things work. My son told me to push the flashing red electronic sensor button, so I did, and after a few minutes the noise finally stopped. I left the cover off and later that night when Jim got home he asked me why it was like that. I told him what had happened and he got a funny look on his face. Then he said, 'That's weird. There haven't been any batteries in this thing for at least six months.'

"Another strange thing that happens at least two or three times a month is that the bathroom water faucet turns itself on full force, so that somebody has to go turn it off. I know the kids aren't doing it, because it's happened when all of us have been sitting in the living room together."

Living in a spooky house would be enough to give anybody bad dreams and both Tamara and her son Chayce have complained of them recently. "I've woken up screaming," she said, "and Chayce has been having a lot of nightmares about bones coming up out of the ground in the garden outside. I don't know if that means anything or not, but I have wondered whether we're built on an old Indian burial ground, or maybe some soldiers died here. We're very close to both the Tongue and the Yellowstone rivers, so who knows? I do know that lots of the strange feelings emanating from this house seem to come from underneath that bedroom where we found the sheepherder's cane. And somehow I just knew intuitively that there had been an archway at one time going into that same room. You couldn't see it anymore, but when we did some remodeling we found it. It had been panelled over and the inside of the arch had been blocked up with wood. When we finally did open it up again, Jim and I both experienced a strange feeling as if a spirit were moving through our bodies."

Tamara and Jim had exhibited psychic sensitivity even before moving into the log house. "The strangest thing happened once when I was walking into another house we owned at the time," Tamara said. "Suddenly, something picked me up about two feet off the ground, turned me completely around in the air, and dropped me flat on my back, so that I was looking up at Jim. Immediately I knew that something had happened to someone I loved. Jim just looked back at me and said, 'Tami, I'm sorry to tell you this, but your grandma just died.' I said, 'I know.'

"Sure enough, the next morning my parents called to tell me that my grandmother had died at five minutes after twelve the night before, at the same time that I had been picked up by that unseen force. And the really odd thing is the way Jim was granted knowledge of my grandmother's death."

Psychic awareness may run in families or, in the case of the Fullers, so many strange things may have happened that even Tamara and Jim's very young children know they're sharing the house with someone who isn't flesh and blood. "We never really talked about this stuff because we didn't want to scare the kids," Tamara explained, "but once when I couldn't find my address book, one of the boys, who was about four at the time, said, 'Well, why don't you just ask the ghost who lives here where it is?' And we hadn't even been here very long when that happened. Both kids have now mentioned the ghost but, fortunately, they don't seem to be afraid. They're just acting like having him around is a normal part of life."

If the boys aren't bothered by the old sheepherder's ghost, the same can't be said for the cat that the Fullers now have. "He looks up at the ceiling and yowls a lot and he's started having accidents on our bed and other things," said Tamara. "And I've started closing the door to that bedroom, since he always seems to want to go in there. I'm not sure that his behavior is caused by the ghost, but who knows?"

Who knows, indeed?

# Nine

......

## Ghosts of the Little Bighorn Battlefield

**W**ithout a doubt, the newly renamed Little Bighorn Battlefield National Monument, in Crow Agency about fifteen miles outside of Hardin, is the most famous haunted location not only in Montana but arguably in the entire western United States. Known previously as Custer Battlefield National Monument, the site has been the center of controversy and mystery ever since Lieutenant Colonel George Armstrong Custer led his ill-fated raid on a village of Lakota Sioux and Cheyenne on a hot Sunday afternoon in June 1876.

Custer and his Seventh Cavalry were part of the U.S. government's campaign to solve what it called the "Indian problem" once and for all. Three separate expeditions, led by George Crook, John Gibbon, and Alfred Terry, were to close in on so-called hostile Sioux who had refused to be herded onto the hated reservations. The plan was for Custer and his troops to march into the valley of the Little Bighorn River and to wait for battalions led by Terry and Gibbon to meet them on June 26.

The reasons why Custer did not wait for the backup troops are still debated. His supporters say that when scout reports told of a large encampment of Sioux, Custer simply wanted to keep the Indians in check before they could escape. He probably also feared that he and his forces had already been sighted by the enemy. Critics charge, however, that since the Democratic Convention was due to be held on June 27, Custer wanted to win a major battle against the Indians in time to be nominated as the presidential candidate. Whatever his reason for haste, on June 25 Custer decided to attack. He divided his forces into three groups, a move that was to prove disastrous.

Captain Frederick Benteen led his soldiers to scout for Indians to the southwest of the encampment, while Major Marcus Reno and his troops went to attack the southern end. Custer and more than two hundred of his men headed north of the Indian village and positioned themselves along the ridge.

When Reno's men began their raid on the unsuspecting village around

......

3:00 P.M., they were dismayed by the fierceness and strength of the Indians, who soon forced their attackers across the river and up into the hills. Almost a third of Reno's troops were dead or missing by the time the rest of them reached the bluffs.

Captain Benteen's forces reached Reno's around 4:15 P.M. and began organizing a defense. But by this time the Indians had already detected Custer's forces near the northern part of the encampment and some had turned their attention away from the counterattack on the southern end to focus attention on the soldiers on the ridge.

In fact, it was probably 3:45 P.M. when Sioux and Cheyenne warriors attacked Custer and his men, overwhelming them with greater numbers and more and better weapons than the Seventh Cavalry knew they had. The battle probably took only an hour or so and at the end Custer and all his men lay dead, many of them mutilated with axes, clubs, and arrows. Some of the wounded who were still conscious could do little but lie in wait as they heard the screams of fellow soldiers being tortured by warriors and even by the Indian women. Worse yet, the injured knew it was inevitable that they themselves would soon be finished off with the same brutal treatment.

When the Sioux and Cheyenne had routed, stripped naked, and dismembered Custer's forces, they returned to lay siege to Reno's and Benteen's men. This fight continued on into the following day and might have gone on longer if the Indians hadn't discovered that Terry's and Gibbon's reinforcements were finally on the way.

Many unanswered questions remain, but what is known is that the Battle of the Little Bighorn claimed approximately two hundred and sixty men from the Seventh Cavalry and an undetermined number of Indians, probably from thirty to one hundred. It is also known that the horrifying events of that June 1876 have so imprinted themselves upon the battlefield that well over a century later they are still causing a wide variety of psychic phenomena.

Even before the battle began, Custer's wife Elizabeth was said to have had a premonition that she would never see her beloved husband again. In a December 1986 *National Geographic* article titled "Ghosts on the Little Bighorn," Robert Paul Jordan says that Libbie's strong sense of impending doom increased as she watched her husband's regiment depart from Fort Lincoln in Dakota Territory. "For as the rising sun played on the mist," Jordan writes, "a mirage had taken form and translated some of the Seventh Cavalry into ghostly horsemen in the sky."

At the same time, Jordan explains, the revered Sioux leader and medicine man Sitting Bull had a vision of "soldiers falling into the Indian camp upside down."

After Libbie's worst fears and Sitting Bull's prophecy were realized and the Battle of the Little Bighorn passed into history, the Crow people, who were the traditional enemies of the Sioux and Cheyenne and whose reservation today surrounds the battlefield, were the first to sense the psychic reverberations from that bloody day. According to Bob Reece's "Visitors of Another Kind," a paper presented to the Boulder Country Corral of Westerners on October 4, 1990, the Crow believed that when the superintendent lowered the flag at the National Cemetery each evening, the spirits were allowed to arise and journey forth. When the flag was raised again the next morning, the souls of the dead returned to their graves. Reece points out that to this day many Crow will not go near the battlefield after dark.

And they certainly aren't the only ones to experience eerie sensations at the site. Reece says that stories of weird happenings told by tourists and employees apparently began in the 1950s. Reece quotes Robert Utley, chief park historian at the battlefield from 1947 to 1952, who insists that there "was no ghost business going on" during his tenure. It seems probable, however, that the phenomena were indeed occurring but were not as widely reported. As Reece points out, Charles Kuhlman, author of *Legend into History* and other works on western themes, was rumored to have visited Last Stand Hill during those years in hopes of contacting Custer's spirit and on at least one occasion to have succeeded. Robert Utley denied that this happened, both to Reece and to me, but the rumor remains.

Utley's successor, James F. Bowers, readily admits that something unsettling happened to him at the visitor center just a few days after he arrived. He mentions the experience in "An Historian Looks at Custer," an article appearing in the November 1966 issue of *The Denver Westerners Monthly Roundup* (vol. 17, no. 10, 4–5):

> When I went to Custer Battlefield National Monument to assume the position of Historian in 1952, accommodations were (and still are) scarce near the site, and as my family wouldn't arrive for several days, I set up a cot and hot plate in the basement of the museum building. Here are stored the hundreds of artifacts, collections, and other donations which have been presented to the government over the last 90

years. By living right in the museum for a few days, I would have at my fingertips the source material necessary to steep myself in the information necessary for my job. During the day I read, asked questions and answered questions, and in the evening I would fix a bite to eat and then gather some material and read until nearly midnight. On about my third night, there I am reading, alone in that big building, with "Custer" all around me, when I hear the front door unlock, open, and someone walk across the floor to the office. Reaching over my head, I opened the door and yelled, "I'm down here." No answer. In a few moments, I heard the footsteps move into the museum area, and once again I hollered that I was down below. The steps cease, but still no answer to my call. When the steps move a third time toward the back door which led to the battlefield and was never unlocked, that was enough for me. I jumped up, locked the door, moved my cot into the darkroom of the photography lab and locked both those doors. There I spent the night and I don't remember that I slept much, either. Later, when I got the nerve to tell my story to the superintendent, he didn't laugh or poke fun at my imagination, but rather left me with the impression that I wasn't the first to have heard General Custer checking the area before turning in for the night.

Bower adds that he regrets not having had the courage to walk up the stairs to confront whoever was there. If his late night visitor really was Custer, Bower suggests, the spirit might have told him what really happened at Last Stand Hill.

Many other employees have also reported strange experiences in the visitor center at the base of this famous hill, but the phenomena have not always involved the ghost of Custer. Stephen Waring from Stoke-on-Trent in England worked as a volunteer in 1984 and he recalls the day in July or August when his friend saw the apparition of Major Edward S. Luce, a man who served in the Seventh Cavalry and who knew some of the men who fought in the Battle of the Little Bighorn.

"My friend was working at the battlefield as an Indian interpreter and he came running upstairs, saying that he had seen a ghost in the visitor center projection room," Stephen remembered. "At first he thought the man he saw was one of the seasonal rangers, but he soon realized that the figure was wearing old-fashioned clothes. My friend looked visibly shaken, and I honestly believe he saw the ghost of Major Luce."

It's hardly surprising that the major would want to remain at the battlefield after death since, following his retirement from the Army, he and his wife Evelyn spent fifteen years publicizing the site and turning it into a tourist attraction.

Stephen Waring himself had some eerie experiences in the same building in the fall of 1984, but he never knew who, or what, was to blame. "Every now and then when I went for a nightly walk, I would return to find all the lights in the visitor center switched on," he explained, "even though a few hours before, I had switched them off. I would turn them off again before leaving, only to have them come on again before everyone arrived for work the next morning. I didn't even try to explain to my supervisor why the lights had been left on all night.

"On another occasion the burglar alarm switched itself on," he continued. "It was set by turning a key clockwise until a red light came on. Once the alarm was set, a one-minute delay allowed everyone to leave the building. After that time, anyone still inside the visitor center would activate the alarm.

"One evening in October or November, between six and seven o'clock, I was finishing some paperwork in the general office. I heard a click which sounded like a key being turned. I don't know why, but I automatically thought of the burglar alarm and, sure enough, it had been switched on. The key was fully turned and the red light was on.

"Anyone in this situation would suspect that someone was playing a practical joke, but I knew full well that everyone else had gone home and I was alone. I made a quick search of the building and then rushed home myself. From then on, I would never stay in the visitor center on my own."

Charles Mulhair was another employee who had a brush with the supernatural in the same building. In the summer of 1988, he worked at the battlefield as a seasonal interpreter and his wife Karol ran the cash register in the museum bookstore. "One day I had just gone down into the book storage room in the southwest corner of the basement," he explained. "I opened the door and turned on the light and, as I did that, I saw a figure with his or her back to me, about fifteen to twenty feet from the door. The person took a step to the left and disappeared down the third aisle, and I wondered why anyone would have been down there in the dark.

"At first I figured it was probably my wife, although everything happened so fast that I couldn't even tell what sex the person was. I said something and walked over to where he or she had been, but I couldn't see anyone. I got a funny feeling and walked out of the room. I doubted myself for a while, but I still recall seeing what was definitely a human form. The person seemed to be wearing a sweater, so maybe that's why I thought it was a woman."

Other employees have reported being physically touched by an invisible phantom. In the summer of 1990, a volunteer was standing behind her desk when she felt someone gently place a hand on her shoulder. She turned around quickly, but no one was there and a check through the offices failed to turn up anyone. An even stranger occurrence the same year was reported by an assistant historian, who felt someone grab his leg when he was giving a program. He looked down and saw no one, but later that day on his way home he suddenly had the urge to veer off in a different direction. Obeying the impulse, he walked through part of the cemetery where he discovered an old cavalry bridle. Ever since, he has wondered whether the two events were in some way connected.

Maintenance men are in an especially likely position to experience odd phenomena at the visitor center since they are so often alone there at all hours of the day and night. Guy Leonard will never forget one early morning in July 1991 when he caught a glimpse of an apparition.

"It must have been about six o'clock, a good two hours before everyone usually comes in," he explained. "I was vacuuming, going from one office to the next, when out of the corner of my eye I saw a person standing about fifteen feet away from me. He was wearing a white, beige, or light brown shirt and he had a black or brown cartridge belt slung diagonally across his chest. I couldn't make out any facial features and he looked a little hazy. I wondered who could be in the building so early in the morning and, as I continued to look at him, he just faded away."

Guy says he wasn't frightened when he saw the phantom soldier, but he admits to having had a weird feeling on other occasions when he heard doors opening and people walking when no one else was in the visitor center. "There's a small swinging door that says 'employees only,'" he said. "Sometimes I hear that thing shut and when I go to see if anyone is there, the building is empty."

Guy was present on another occasion in the summer of 1991 when a staff member heard a phantom voice from the theater downstairs. "We were getting ready to hold a CPR class in there," Guy recalled, "and one of the rangers asked this guy, 'Hey, Joe, are you going to take the CPR class again this year?' Joe answered, 'Yeah,' and went on downstairs to open up the back door leading into the theater. He and one of the medics out of Hardin were bringing in some gear for the class and when they were both at one end of the room they heard a voice repeat, 'Hey, Joe, are you going to take that class this year?' Joe turned around to look, but could see no one. He asked the medic if he had spoken and the medic answered that he thought Joe had said something. Neither man had asked the question, but they both heard it. And they were sure that no one else was there.

"The creepy thing is that a tourist actually died of a heart attack right there in the theater two or three years ago," Guy explained. "So maybe his ghost wanted to make sure that Joe kept brushing up on his CPR techniques for the benefit of other people, even though it was too late to save him."

While a number of spooky things have taken place in the visitor center, even more have occurred in what is called the Stone House, built in 1894 as a residence for the superintendent of the National Cemetery. Now used to house summer staff at the battlefield, the two-story building is located beside the entrance gate to the vast graveyard, established in 1879, where among the thousands of dead are soldiers from other Indian battles and conflicts as recent as the Vietnam war.

The oldest standing building in Big Horn County, the Stone House is considered by Bob Reece and others who have spent time there to be the center of supernatural activity at the Little Bighorn Battlefield. Perhaps this is only to be expected, since the basement of the structure was at one time used to store bodies before they were buried in the adjacent cemetery.

"Lights are frequently seen burning in different parts of the Stone House when the building is known to be empty," said Michael Moore, who began working as a living history interpreter in 1984. "During winter weather it's especially eerie when the lights come on, because often there are no tracks in the snow leading up to the place."

According to Bob Reece's paper, one former chief historian who lived on the battlefield during the winter reported that he often saw lights burning in the upstairs apartment of the Stone House. He always went to turn them off, but on one occasion he couldn't get the front door to open. Frustrated, he went home and returned an hour later, at which time the door opened easily.

Probably the strangest incident involving a light on in the Stone House occurred in 1980, on a mid-spring evening around sunset. Historian Mardell Plainfeather was returning to the battlefield after visiting some relatives when she noticed a light burning on the second story. She was well aware of the weird reputation of the Stone House, but since it was the time of year when housing for summer employees was being spruced up, she decided that the light probably had been left on by maintenance personnel.

Mardell stopped at the apartment of Mike and Ruth Massie, about two hundred yards below the Stone House, to ask Mike to go with her to turn off the light. Because Mardell had her small daughter with her, Mike volunteered to do the job himself.

"I went up the stairs of the old place and looked around to see if anyone was there," Mike recalled. "I couldn't see anybody, so I went on up to the second floor to flip the light switch off. As I started walking back to my apartment, my wife Ruth ran outside and I could see that she was shaken up.

"She had been watching television on a used set we had just bought in a repair shop in Hardin and, at the same time I was upstairs in the Stone House, a strange voice had suddenly spoken through the TV, saying only the words 'second floor.' Ruth knew that I was on the second floor of the Stone House and she wondered if everything was all right. We never could figure out why that eerie voice came out of the television, or what it meant."

Michael Moore was equally puzzled by some strange occurrences in the Stone House on a night in May 1989. "My roommate Michael Donahue and I had just finished a camp of instruction in Fort Laramie, Wyoming, and it was our first or second night back at the battlefield," he explained. "We were staying in the front room; a maintenance man sometimes stayed in the back room, but he wasn't there that night. I was still up reading and Mike had already fallen asleep.

"Between our room and the back room was a padlocked door. Suddenly I heard a noise as if someone were pushing on it and trying to get out. At first I thought I might have been imagining things, but then I heard it again a minute or so later. Mike was still asleep and I decided that the next time I heard the banging I'd wake him up to find out for sure whether anybody was staying in that back room.

"When the pounding began again, I tried to wake Mike to ask him, but he was so tired that he just mumbled something and went back to sleep. The sound came again two or three more times in the next five minutes and the last two bangs were really loud. I never did figure out what was causing this to happen—it wasn't even a windy night."

About sixteen months later, in September 1990, Michael Moore heard even stranger noises in the Stone House. "I was living there alone and

The Stone House, considered by many to be the center of supernatural activity at the Little Bighorn Battlefield. (*Photograph courtesy Little Bighorn Battlefield National Monument*)

I was up around midnight doing my laundry," he recalled. "The utility room was in a building about seventy-five yards away and I was carrying my clothes back home when I heard a noise like a door slamming somewhere inside the house.

"I thought that was odd since I was the only one living there, but I wondered whether a friend had dropped by to see me. I looked all over the house, but no one was there. I returned downstairs to fold my clothes and after about ten minutes I heard the sound of something heavy, such as a file cabinet, being turned over on either the second floor or up in the attic. This banging sound continued for an hour or two and I also heard what sounded like someone jumping off the couch upstairs and walking around.

"There's a door at the top of the stairs and I could also hear its handle turning," Mike continued. "Just a day or so before I heard these things a maintenance man had been working on the roof and one of the chemicals he was using started a fire. The blaze was quickly extinguished, but I wondered whether it somehow triggered all the activity I heard upstairs."

Regardless of the cause of the sounds, other people have also heard them. "Former staff member Joe Albertson and his wife Louise [not their real names] have spent many summers in the Stone House since the 1950s and they've heard and actually seen the door handle turning," Mike told me. "They've also heard the heavy thing being pushed over somewhere upstairs, as did a maintenance man in 1991. This guy also heard people screaming and children talking inside the building."

In addition to hearing mysterious noises inside the Stone House, people have sighted apparitions there. Some have supposedly seen the ghost of Major Luce peering from the small round window at the top of the house and, according to Bob Reece's paper, others have seen an unidentified woman's figure descending the stairs. Reece and Michael Moore were both told the story of a new battlefield ranger who was staying in an upstairs apartment of the Stone House. On his first night, he awoke and felt someone sit down on the end of his bed. At first he thought the person was his wife, until he remembered that she was away visiting her family. As the ranger reached for the Colt .45 lying on his nightstand, he was able to make out the shadowy form moving from the foot of his bed. As he continued to watch, he saw the torso of a soldier, minus the head and legs, move quickly across the room until it disappeared into an adjoining one.

The sighting of incomplete apparitions is not unusual, since it apparently takes an incredible amount of energy for one to appear at all. Ghost lore is replete with phantoms who look as if they have everything but a head, a right foot, or legs from the knees down, for example—and in most cases they appear this way not because their original physical bodies were similarly deficient, but because they lack enough energy for a complete materialization. In the case of apparitions at the Little Bighorn Battlefield, there may be another, albeit ghastly, reason why they do not appear entire.

When the forces of Terry and Gibbon arrived at the scene of the battle, they were sickened by the bloated and mutilated corpses of Custer's troops. Custer's brother Thomas, for example, had been so horribly butchered that his body was identifiable only by a tattoo on his arm. Indian drawings depicting the slaughter also show clearly that the remains of many of the slain were beheaded and otherwise dismembered, and archeological examination of some of the skeletons proved that this kind of mutilation occurred. Is it not possible, then, that such horrific treatment of a body could cause its apparition to also appear in pieces?

But what caused the materialization of an Indian man in the bedroom on the top floor of the Stone House? Dan Martinez, now an historian at the Arizona Memorial Museum Association in Hawaii, still doesn't know what to make of an experience he had when he was a seasonal ranger and interpreter at the Little Bighorn Battlefield from 1979 to 1985.

"I admit that when I was a seasonal there, I used to make up scary stories about the Stone House so that other people would be afraid of it," he said. "That way, I could be sure of staying in the old place myself. I really enjoyed my time there and I never believed in such things as ghosts. But one night I experienced something I've never been able to explain. I don't know whether it was a dream or an actual occurrence, but if it was just a dream, it seemed terribly real.

"I think it was June 1982, and I remember waking up one night to find someone standing over me, right next to my side of the bed. It was a moonlit night and I saw without a doubt that this person was an Indian and he was just standing there and staring down at me.

"I was absolutely powerless to move or to wake my wife lying beside me. I couldn't even speak as I watched this man. At first I thought he was a real person, because he looked absolutely solid and was dressed in all the trappings of an American Indian. Most notable was an eagle feather hanging off to one side of his head. I could barely breathe and I felt as if there were a huge depression on my chest.

"My bed was against the wall and there was a doorway no more than three or four feet away. I still couldn't move, but my eyes rolled to watch as the man turned to walk out of the room. After he left, my heart was pounding and I was perspiring profusely, even though it was a cool night. I was just frozen with terror and it took me a while before I was able to wake up my wife.

"The whole experience lasted no more than a minute, but it seemed an eternity and had a profound effect on me, especially since I used to joke with others about their belief in the supernatural. To this day, the most disturbing thing about what happened is that I don't know whether it was a dream or reality."

Although the phantom in Dan Martinez's bedroom seemed menacing, at least one spirit in the Stone House has apparently acted in a benevolent way. Joe and Louise Albertson frequently experienced unexplainable occurrences during their many summers in the house, including footsteps from the empty upstairs and objects being mysteriously moved around. According to Bob Reece's paper, one day just as Louise was about to eat lunch, she heard a loud, high-pitched noise coming from the kitchen. It sounded like the whistle of a tea kettle, but no kettle was boiling at the time. Louise was just about to take her first bite when the whistle sounded louder. Perceiving that she was being warned about something, Louise looked at her lunch, which included some leftover chicken. She decided that it had spoiled and threw it away, feeling grateful to the spirit who might have saved her from food poisoning.

When Guy Leonard worked as a seasonal interpreter at the battlefield, he stayed for a while in the Stone House and never encountered anything out of the ordinary. But one day not long after he began working as a maintenance man in January 1991, he was sweeping and stacking boxes in the basement of the old house when he heard the sound of someone clearing his throat.

"My first thought was that my supervisor had come in and was trying to let me know he was there without startling me," Guy said. "I stopped and looked around, but no one was in the room; so I went over to the door that went upstairs. I checked everywhere and no one else was in the house. I even looked out the window and saw that there was only one set of footprints leading to the Stone House—and it was mine."

Not long afterward, on a night in March or April 1991, Guy's wife Janet was walking over by the Stone House to take a picture of the moon through the pine trees over the cemetery. As she lined up her shot to get the best picture, she heard someone say, "Hey, you there!"

Janet spun around, expecting to find a certain ranger who was staying at the battlefield during the spring season. She saw nobody, but she noticed lights on in the ranger's apartment a short distance away. She walked around the Stone House looking for the person who had spoken to her, but she found no one. Thinking that perhaps a tourist might have parked a car by the main gates and walked in, she went to check, but there was no car and no sign of another person. Later, Janet learned that the ranger and his wife had been sitting in their living room watching TV at the time she heard the voice.

Employee living quarters other than the Stone House have also been the setting for psychic phenomena. Tim Bernardis, who came to the battlefield in 1983 as a participant in the Volunteer in the Parks program, lived in Apartment D, where he often awoke to see a figure standing at the foot of his bed. The sighting of "hypnagogic" images when one is in the stage between wakefulness and sleep is fairly common and is a little understood function of the brain. Tim continues to see these "bedroom invaders" even away from the battlefield, but he had the experience most often while he was there.

"When I saw the figures, I'd shout, get up, and turn on the light," he said. "One roommate said I used to yell things like 'Get out of here' and 'What's going on?' But when I started leaving the door to my room open, I didn't see the images anymore—at least not while I was at the battlefield. I guess I felt safer with the door open."

Bob Reece was another participant in the Volunteer in the Parks program and he had an unusual experience one June night in the mid-1980s when he was staying with Doug Keller in Apartment A. "Douglas Ellison had also come to visit for a week or so," Bob recalled, "and early one morning, around three o'clock, I awoke to the sound of someone walking down the road from the direction of the Stone House. The person had a heavy step and was wearing boots. I assumed it was Ellison because he's a big guy over six feet tall and well built. The footsteps came closer and, just before they reached the apartment building, they stopped.

"By then I was wide awake. I listened for the sound of someone entering one of the other three apartments, which normally would have been impossible not to hear. No one went into any of them, however, and we found out later that Doug Ellison had ended up spending the night in Hardin. Doug Keller slept through the whole thing and I never heard the footsteps again after they stopped so abruptly."

A night or two later, Douglas Ellison heard the same mystery person strolling outside. "I had been out late with a local girl and when I returned to the apartment it was probably a little past midnight," he said. "The others were asleep until I came barging in, wide awake and talkative and, after five or ten minutes, they finally told me to shut up.

"I lay down on the floor in a comfortable spot and tried to sleep," Doug continued. "It must have been half an hour later when from outside I heard the sound of someone in heavy boots walking toward the apartment building. I figured it was just some guy coming home late as I had done; his heavy stride continued for perhaps seven or eight seconds, getting closer all the time. Then the walking just stopped.

"What gave me a start was that no lock turned, no door opened or closed, and no footsteps led away. I lay awake for at least another half hour and I heard not one more sound from outside. The next day I asked other people staying in the apartments if they had heard anything or been out late and they all said they hadn't."

On another hot summer night in the same apartment, Doug Keller was reading in bed when someone knocked on his door. "By the time I got out of bed, put my pants on, and opened the door, no one was there," he recalled. "I didn't think there was anything especially unusual about that, except that the next day I couldn't get anyone to admit that he or she had dropped by."

Seasonal worker Chris Summit recalls another strange incident that took place in Apartment A one winter night in the early 1980s. "I was a good friend of former chief historian Neil Mangum, who was also living on the battlefield," Chris explained. "There was quite a path in the snow between our two places, since I was always going to play video games and battle games on maps with him.

"Neil generally laughed at all this supernatural business, but that winter we enjoyed telling each other scary stories. One night I left his place late and trudged back through the snow to my apartment. I went to bed as soon as I got home. With my bedroom door open, I could look into the living room adjoining the kitchen.

"I'd been asleep for a while, when suddenly I woke up," Chris continued. "At that same instant, I saw the light come on in the kitchen. Immediately, I thought of all the spooky stories Neil and I had been telling each other and I figured he had come into my apartment and was playing a trick on me.

"I got out of bed and crept to the corner of the kitchen, then I sprang out crying, 'Boo!' to scare whoever was there. But there was nobody in the room. I checked the doors, but they were all locked.

"I turned the light off and went back to bed, thinking that the light switch must have gotten stuck or something. But the next morning I examined it and discovered that it was the kind that turns either all the way on or off with a hard click. I also checked to make sure that the light bulb wasn't screwed in loosely so that a sudden vibration would make it come on."

If paranormal energy caused the light to behave strangely, it might also have been the reason for an odd occurrence in Charles and Karol Mulhair's travel trailer in 1989. An archeological dig was conducted that year at the site where Reno was believed to have dumped extra supplies after backup forces arrived on the twenty-seventh of June. An earlier excavation following a fire in 1983 had yielded much new information about Custer's battle and the soldiers who died in it, but the later dig was largely a failure. The only high point was a volunteer's discovery of a human clavicle, humerus, and skull poking from the roots of a tree along the bank of the Little Bighorn, at the precise location where the Indians forced Reno's troops across the river and up into the hills.

According to Andrew Ward's article, "The Little Bighorn," published in the April 1992 issue of *American Heritage*, a forensic sculptor used the skull to produce a bust of the cavalryman and the trooper's identity was narrowed to two possibilities. Although the identification is not archeologically conclusive at the time of this writing, the unfortunate soldier was almost certainly Sergeant Edward Botzer of Company G. The bust made by the forensic sculptor looked so much like Botzer's relatives that the family claimed the remains and buried them at the National Cemetery on June 23, 1991.

The Mulhairs recall the excitement at the battlefield when the soldier's remains were found. "That night, the archeologists had a little wine and cheese party to show off the skull and everybody went to see it," Charles said. "Afterward, Karol and I came back to our trailer. When she went to bed, I turned off the television and started to go back to the bedroom. Suddenly, the TV came on by itself—something it has never done at any other time before or since. We decided that the ghost of the cavalryman was trying to tell us something, but I'm not sure what it was—maybe he just wasn't finished watching the news."

One of the most uncanny occurrences ever reported at the battlefield took place in 1983 when Christine Hope was a student intern living in Apartment C. Because no one at the site knows Christine's current whereabouts, I was unable to contact her, but her story is told in "Visions of Reno Crossing," a chapter in Earl Murray's *Ghosts of the Old West*.

The summer season had ended and there were fewer tourists, so Chris Hope and Tim Bernardis decided that they finally had time to visit the Reno Retreat Crossing, the area where the Sioux counterattacked Reno's troops, forcing them across the river and up onto the bluffs. After finalizing plans to go the following afternoon, Chris and Tim returned to their apartments for the evening.

Chris's apartment was arranged as a small efficiency unit and she customarily slept either on the sofa or on a mattress or sleeping bag on the living room floor. In the middle of the night before she was due to visit Reno Crossing, she awoke suddenly and saw the figure of a man sitting in one of her living room chairs.

Terrified and unable to speak, Chris stared at the man for quite some time. His face was illuminated by a moonbeam shining through a window across from the couch and by its light Chris was able to make out the man's light-colored beard and long, flowing handlebar mustache. As Chris continued to study the man, she realized that he was not from the twentieth century. She had seen photographs of the men who fought in the Battle of the Little Bighorn and this man looked as if he belonged to the same era.

It began to dawn on Chris that she was seeing a ghost, but what alarmed her even more was the expression of horror on the man's face. "It was his eyes that got to me the most," Murray quotes Chris as saying. "It's hard to explain, but those eyes stood out. They were filled with incredible fright. The moon shone on them and they were filled with terror." Chris finally blinked her eyes and when she opened them again the chair was empty and the apparition was gone.

The next afternoon, as planned, she and Tim Bernardis visited the site of Reno Crossing. As they walked along the bluffs and the riverbank, Tim explained the details of the action that occurred on the day of the battle, emphasizing that those who were unscathed at the beginning of the counterattack tried to drag the dead and wounded with them up into the hills. At one spot near the Little Bighorn River, Tim and Chris paused at a lone marker with the name of Second Lieutenant Benjamin H. Hodgson inscribed on it. The marker indicated the approximate place where Hodgson's body had been found.

After their tour of Reno Crossing, Tim and Chris returned to the visitor center where they looked through an out-of-print book with pictures and military histories of the soldiers who died at the Battle of the Little Bighorn. When they came to Hodgson's photograph, Chris was unable to conceal her shock and blurted out, "That's the person I saw in my room last night!"

Earl Murray's account goes on to explain that Lieutenant Hodgson had one of the slowest and most harrowing deaths of any of the cavalrymen who died during Reno's retreat. Survivors of the battle recalled that as Hodgson forded the river, a bullet shattered his leg and killed his horse, but he was still able to grab at a stirrup kicked out at him by another soldier. Wounded and in shock, Hodgson was then dragged through the river to the other side. In spite of his agony, he tried to crawl up the steep embankment, but made it only part of the way before being shot and killed by another bullet. His body then rolled back down the bank toward the water.

Murray notes that when Chris Hope learned about the fate of Lieutenant Hodgson, the man who was well liked by Reno's men and whose

Second Lieutenant Benjamin H. Hodgson, before he grew a beard and handlebar mustache. (*Photo courtesy Little Bighorn Battlefield National Monument*)

nickname was "Benny," she understood the tragic message his tortured eyes had been trying to convey—that what had happened to the combatants in the Battle of the Little Bighorn should never happen to human beings of any race and that no one should ever treat lightly the horror of June 25 and 26, 1876.

As Chris told her story to more people, she learned that she was not the first to have been contacted by the ghost of Lieutenant Hodgson. A few years earlier, one man had apparently seen the head of the soldier enveloped in a white gaseous cloud, which hovered over the percipient's bed the night before he too visited Reno Crossing. And according to Bob Reece, only a year after Hodgson died, his spirit had attempted to communicate with a friend, Lieutenant Clinton H. Tebbetts. This communication, which came through a medium, stated simply that the Seventh Cavalry had fought gallantly. The incident was reported by the late John M. Carroll in the November 1988 *Newsletter* published by the Little Bighorn Associates.

Although many weird occurrences have been reported in various buildings at the battlefield, it's hardly surprising that paranormal phenomena have also taken place at the actual sites where the fighting occurred and where the dead fell and were buried.

"The battlefield is a spooky place, especially at night," Doug Keller admitted. "The National Cemetery and the markers of the soldiers who were killed in the Battle of the Little Bighorn are very eerie and you can scare yourself easily if you have an overactive imagination."

Some might say that just such an overactive imagination was at work when a tourist from New Orleans claimed to have been transported back in time to the day of the battle, or when a cab driver from Minneapolis saw soldiers and Indians engaged in a fight to the death on a ridge. And it may be just a coincidence that the only roll of film photographer Cliff Soubier ever lost had a picture of historian Jerome Green on the battlefield, holding a Ouija board.

"If the film had been lost at the processor's, that would not have been unusual," Cliff pointed out. "But I process my own black and white shots, so I can't imagine what happened."

Cliff Nelson has worked seasonally at the battlefield since the late 1960s and although he's never experienced anything out of the ordinary himself, he knows that many of those who have are very credible people, not the type to exaggerate or to imagine things. On an evening in August 1976, for example, a no-nonsense National Park Service law enforcement officer visited the Last Stand site and, as he looked out over the mass grave where most of the dead from the battle now repose, he felt a sudden drop in temperature and heard the soft murmuring of many voices. The feeling of oppression grew so strong that he was finally forced to leave.

And then, thirteen or fourteen years ago, there was the experience of Mardell Plainfeather, a Crow and the former Plains Indian historian at the battlefield. Mardell had granted permission for a Crow medicine man to use her private sweat lodge near the river.

"It takes a long, long time to make a good sweat lodge," Mardell explained. "You have to build a fire to heat the stones and then you haul the stones to a hole in the ground to make a sauna-like effect. Native Americans use the sweat lodge to pray and to cleanse themselves spiritually, and the medicine man had a special prayer to offer that day.

"He was finished around six-thirty in the evening and he came by to say that even though he had put out the fire I should probably check later to make sure that the wind hadn't fanned the flames and restarted a blaze. I assured him that I would, but I became interested in a TV special and forgot about checking the sweat lodge until after I had gone to bed.

"I didn't want to get up and I told myself that surely the fire was out, but I kept imagining the whole valley ablaze. Finally, I decided to make sure that everything was okay. I didn't want to leave my little girl by herself, so I woke her up and we drove down to the sweat lodge. I shone a light on the fire and, sure enough, a small flame was still flickering.

"I kicked the ground, poured dirt on the fire, and took a stick to knock it out," Mardell continued. "A lot of ash was stirred up and I knew I had to get some water on the flames, but I didn't want to get it from the river. I was alone with my child and what if I fell in?

"We drove back to the house, where I got a jug of water and took it back to douse the fire. When it was safely extinguished, I got in the car and backed out of the brush and overgrowth in front of the sweat lodge. Then, out of the corner of my eye, I saw something on top of the bluff.

"I stopped the car and turned around in my seat to look. I rolled my window down, stuck my head out, and saw clearly that something was moving up there. At first I thought that one of the summer rangers was playing a trick on me, because we were always doing that to each other.

"I didn't hear any noise, so I got out of the car to see more clearly. And there, up on the bluffs with the bright night sky behind them, were the silhouettes of two Indian warriors on horseback.

"At first I couldn't believe my eyes," Mardell continued. "For one thing, horses aren't even allowed on the battlefield. I rubbed my eyes and looked again as one of the warriors lifted himself up on his horse, moving his head from side to side to get a better look at me. One had flowing hair and the other had braids and they both wore feathers. One had a shield on his back and I could see that the other carried a spear and had a bow and quiver behind him.

"I looked inside the car and could tell that my daughter had seen the horsemen too. I jumped back in and drove home, praying all the while that we wouldn't get stuck in the brushy road. When I got home, though, I was surprised to discover how calm I felt.

"The next morning I took a cigarette and some sweet smelling sage to the place where I had seen the warriors," Mardell said. "There was nothing there that I could possibly have mistaken for two men on horseback and there was no trace of horses having been on the bluff. I offered a smoke and left the twig of sage behind."

Mardell's Crow tribe was on the Army's side during the battle and Custer even had Crow scouts. But Mardell's job at the battlefield was to explain to visitors the Sioux and Cheyenne side of the story. "I believe that the warriors just wanted to see this Crow woman who was trying to do justice to their point of view," she explained. "I believe that they appeared in order to express their approval of what I was doing."

A highly sensationalized version of Mardell's experience was published in the *National Enquirer,* but an accurate account appeared later in the *National Geographic* article. Sioux sculptor and artist R. G. Bowker read about Mardell's vision and in its honor she created a sculpture of the two warriors on horseback.

I've always had strong feelings for the battleground," Ms. Bowker told me, "and I believe there were forces working to bring all this about."

Psychics visiting the battlefield have long been aware of those forces, or at least of vibrations from the tragic past. Bob Reece writes of a moonless night in August 1987 when a psychic from Colorado visited the site for the first time. Although she knew little about the facts of the battle, she was able to provide concrete details of what occurred at Medicine Tail Ford and Nye-Cartwright Ridge. At the site of "Custer's Last Stand," she claimed to feel the presence of at least a third of the spirits from the slaughtered battalion.

"The Warrior Spirits of Victory at the Little Big Horn," R. G. Bowker's sculptural interpretation of historian Mardell Plainfeather's vision. (*Photo courtesy R. G. Bowker*)

Reece goes on to say that, at the cemetery, the psychic saw a ghostly warrior charge a seasonal employee, touch him to count coup, then turn and ride past the visitor center and down Cemetery Ridge. The employee had been resting, his eyes closed, but when the warrior rode past him the drowsy man reportedly opened his eyes and asked, "What was that?"

Behind the seasonal workers' dwellings, the psychic also saw twenty to thirty warriors painted and dressed for war, with feathers pointed down from their heads. Reece wonders whether these might not have been the small group known as "the suicide boys," who entered the fighting when it was almost over and sacrificed themselves for the good of their people.

The most fascinating as well as the most accomplished psychic connected with the site is Howard R. Starkel, who assisted in a series of experiments with Dr. Don Rickey, former historian at the battlefield.

By means of psychometry, the practice of "reading" vibrations from inanimate objects in an attempt to learn more about the people who owned them, Starkel and Dr. Rickey have achieved astonishing results, detailed first in *The Courier*, a National Park Service publication, and later in the spring 1986 issue of *Applied Psi*.

In the *Applied Psi* article, "In Touch with the Past: Experiments in Psychometry at Custer Battlefield," Rickey explains the theory behind the technique:

> Moments of high emotional intensity can leave their imprint on objects long after their human users have gone. Yet these objects can be like reels of old movie footage, useless without a projector. . . . *Psychometry* brings object and psychic together in order to unlock the imprints of the past. The psychic serves as the projector, so to speak; he or she holds and concentrates on a tin can, a bit of shoe leather, a rusted iron spur, whatever object may have been associated with a moment of intense emotion, and projects impressions made by the passing of a previous owner.

Upon examination, psychometry doesn't seem so farfetched. A law of physics, after all, is that every living entity gives off electromagnetic field impulses, psychic traces that remain on objects even after the entity's death. In July 1979, Dr. Rickey gave Howard Starkel a rusted iron spur supposedly found in the Little Bighorn Valley somewhere in the vicinity of the battlefield. Starkel was told nothing about the spur, including where it had been found, and he knew almost nothing about the geography of the area or details about the Battle of the Little Bighorn. In fact, he had almost no knowledge of the way Indian wars were fought. And yet, by taking the spur in his hands, closing his eyes, and concentrating upon the object for five to ten seconds, Starkel spoke, giving the following information about the owner of the spur:

> I was hurt; this was found in a desolate area; I am with other people. . . . Trees were nearby, in a valley—there is emotion . . . hurry, startled, want to get on horseback, close to a stream, where all my activity was starting, trying to get to horseback. I have been hurt, and want to get across the stream to a hill to defend myself, about 150 yards away from the stream. I want to take off a black boot—I think I was shot, and am in pain but still running. . . . We're just a group, but not the big group. Attackers pulled back. I am crossing the stream with a

few others. The larger group is elsewhere. I am a big man, but have
no hat. The people chasing me . . . one has a bull's-eye painted on his
chest—they are mounted. I feel directionally disoriented. I go across
the stream—this spur was lost on the south side just after I crossed the
stream to climb the high ridges, in a panic to leave. I want to go across
the river and north, to a main body, but can't. The enemies have backed
away; they don't have time to play with us. They go back to fight the
main body going to the northwest. Horses lost at the river; are there
horse carcasses? I see a fire, away from the object. The owner did not
make it through the battle.

Amazingly, Starkel's comments correlated with known historical
information concerning Reno's retreat and they seemed to refer specifically
to one J. M. DeWolf, a civilian contract surgeon who was killed east
of the river at that time. Dr. Rickey points out that as a civilian, DeWolf
would have had to outfit himself and thus would very likely not have
worn the regulation Army brass spurs. Starkel's comments are also consistent with the fact that DeWolf's marker is about two-thirds of the way
up a ridge from the river to the defense site. And Starkel's reference to
a fire is consistent with historical facts, for the Indians set ablaze the
grass in the valley when they left the battlefield.

Starkel was given other objects to examine, including a .50 Martin
primed Army shell case. The bullet apparently had been fired by an
Indian, "kneeling and shooting—not too far from water." Starkel goes
on to say that the Indian was angry and grief-stricken over the recent
death of his wife, for which he blamed the Army. The psychic then
describes the soldiers, both mounted and on foot, milling around in a
confused state with no leadership apparent. Then he narrates the actions
of the Indian who fired the bullet:

The user is not rapid firing—he doesn't have much ammunition—
a careful user of ammunition. He accounted for three soldiers here—
he wasn't more than 50–60 yards from the soldiers, and other Indians
are up closer to the soldiers—some mounted. He was a marksman, but
the recoil hurts his shoulder. . . . He has long leggins [*sic*] on, no feathers
I can see . . . [hair] divided into three braids. Firing this weapon, there
is something like a back blast—it is not like a Springfield carbine. . . . At
one point, a lot of Indians leave the fighting area (the mounted men)
and go northward. . . . The shell user stays in the same place or area,
and is still there at the end. The shell user walks away when the shooting

stops—he is looking over his own casualties—scattered. Some scavenging is going on, for weapons and ammunition. An occasional shot is heard. He went through the saddle bags on a dead horse. . . . His shoulder is sore from shooting. The length of the battle was not long, but it was intense.

Neil Mangum, chief historian at the time the experiments were conducted, writes an afterword to the article in which he admits that reading Rickey's report about the iron spur "sent chills racing" up his spine. When Starkel actually came to the site to do further experiments, Neil Mangum was "stunned" by the psychic's high degree of accuracy, and his afterword suggests that while psychometry will never replace the standard methodology, it nevertheless has too much "inexplicable truth" to be passed off as fake and fraudulent.

Indeed, one value of psychometry is that it emphasizes the "human element" of history—the emotions, motivations, pain, and longing of real people playing their part in the unfolding of events. And no one today has a better understanding than Doug Keller of what it must have felt like to die at the Little Bighorn Battlefield. After spending at least six summers and one winter at the site, Doug has given the matter a lot of thought.

"The thing that brings about the demise of the physical body is always shocking, and dying in combat is not like dying at home or dying from an illness," he explained. "The Battle of the Little Bighorn was an extremely violent situation and there was a tremendous cultural difference involved, with European Americans fighting Native Americans. A lot of the soldiers who fought were very young, still in their teens, and many were immigrants who weren't even born in the United States. Separated from their homes and families, they must have been very lonely—and then they were suddenly and unexpectedly killed, many years before their time.

"You'd expect a certain anger, bitterness, or frustration on their part. Imagine how any of us would feel about dying young, leaving our families so early and wondering what would happen to them. If we assume that feelings can linger, it's no wonder that the battlefield is haunted."

Doug is sure that the feelings of the Sioux and Cheyenne warriors were much the same as those of the soldiers, and the Indians faced the additional threat of losing their lands, their freedoms—their entire way of life.

If there is a lesson to be learned from the events of June 1876, it's that people simply cannot afford to kill each other—the psychic cost of war is too high. This message was proclaimed cosmically, in the heavens themselves on the one hundredth anniversary of the Battle of the Little Bighorn.

Former seasonal ranger and historian Dan Martinez was commemorating the centennial with a group of historians and artists. They were riding toward Medicine Tail Coulee, a natural crossing which at the time of the battle led into the northern end of the Indian village. It's still open to question whether Custer's forces ever reached the Coulee; if they did, they disappeared into history shortly thereafter.

"The day of the centennial was rainy with strange atmospheric conditions," Dan Martinez recalled. "And as we were riding, one cloud before us literally rose up in a plume and formed into the shape of an Indian coup stick, similar to a large cane with a curved hook and feathers dangling off the end. As the warriors rode by their enemies, they would touch them, or "count coup," with the sticks. Such a custom actually demonstrated more bravery than killing their foes.

"Everybody there that day saw this shape in the sky. It hung suspended in the air, directly over the battlefield. And, suddenly, sunlight broke through the clouds and shone right on Last Stand Hill at the same moment. It was an incredible sight and everyone who saw it knew that they'd shared something special."

What was the meaning of this sign from above? Could it have appeared to show us that it takes more courage to try to understand our enemies than to kill them, no matter which side we're on? If so, then that's the most important lesson anyone could ever learn at the Little Bighorn Battlefield National Monument.

# Ten

## The Mystery of the House in Philipsburg

Judith Petersen and her grown children Frances and James (not their real names) were in the market for some real estate in the early 1970s and they couldn't believe the wonderful deal they were getting on the old house in Philipsburg. The gorgeous two-and-a-half-story Victorian structure was in remarkably good condition and its oak floors and woodwork, beautifully designed staircases, and ornate brass fittings made the property a steal at only five thousand dollars.

The Petersens also liked the "old" feeling of the little town of Philipsburg and they planned to use the house on weekends, when they would drive down from Missoula. Frances also planned to stay there during the summer to write her thesis and later they could rent out the house for extra income.

Even though the place was in good shape, the Petersens still had work to do before it was ready to live in. One Saturday afternoon they drove down to begin fixing it up, bringing sixteen-year-old Paul along to help. They worked steadily all afternoon and well into the evening but, for some reason, as soon as it got dark they began to feel uncomfortable.

"We had brought our sleeping bags so we could spend the night in the house, but when it came time to use them nobody wanted to go upstairs," Judith explained. "Even though the living room didn't have any curtains on the windows at that time, I suggested that we'd probably be more comfortable there since it was downstairs.

"I'll never forget the steady stream of cars that passed by the house that first night, almost as if people were curious to see how we were doing," she continued. "I tried to rest, but I couldn't stop feeling nervous. Being a good Catholic, I said my prayers, asking for protection for the house and for us. Finally, I got to sleep."

The next morning Paul went upstairs to explore the attic. There was no furniture there except for a small potbellied stove, but what caught Paul's attention were old papers stuffed underneath some boards. "I found a receipt for a livery hack used during a funeral and a letter informing someone about a woman's death," he remembered. "Apparently she died after falling down the stairs from a back bedroom into the kitchen. The letter also said that she had gotten rather difficult to live with in her old age and, as I recall, some references were made to her being a concert musician, perhaps a pianist."

The Petersens don't recall the year the woman was supposed to have died, but they believe it must have been between 1890 and 1910. Frances thought she remembered that the letter was addressed to a man in St. Louis and that the woman might also have been from there; Judith remembered something to the effect that the woman and the people with whom she lived had met each other at a fair in Chicago.

The Petersens had told their story earlier to D. F. Curran for his *True Hauntings in Montana* and I'm using the same pseudonyms that appear there. Curran's account says that the woman musician had been taken in by the male owner of the house and that because he had taken care of her funeral arrangements, he considered anything she had owned while living there to be his.

"It seemed strange that these papers were the only things left in the attic and that they had apparently been sitting there for about seventy years," James told me. "They had an eerie effect on us, but we went ahead and spent the rest of the day working on the house. When it got dark, however, we knew we didn't want to spend another night there."

Judith decided to take the letter and the hearse receipt, because she wanted to write a story for the newspaper based on the incidents described in them. But on the way home in the car, Frances was suddenly startled by an unfamiliar face looking back at her from the front windshield and James was equally disturbed to see what looked like a pair of eyes between his brother and sister in the back seat.

"I may have been a little overwrought, but at the time I was sure of what I saw," he insisted. "We were all jumpy and we wondered whether the letter and the hearse receipt were the cause of our bad feelings. Just to be safe, we threw them both out the window."

Even with the strange documents no longer in their possession, the Petersens still had the sensation that someone or something had followed them home. Too scared to sleep in separate rooms, they all decided to sleep together in the living room just as they'd done in the house in Philipsburg. But no one slept peacefully and Paul had a nightmare that an entity of some kind was trying to get inside of him.

"When I awakened, I woke my mother and told her I was frightened,"

Paul said, "and about a minute afterward we heard a sudden blast of music coming from somewhere in the house. It sounded just like someone had turned the volume way up on some classical music for a few seconds. We couldn't figure out where it was coming from or what caused it in the first place. We were on edge anyway, and this incident scared us so much that we said a prayer together."

A similar incident happened at the house in Philipsburg when James and some hunting buddies were there. "I hadn't said anything to my friends about our weird experiences because I didn't want them to think I was an idiot," James explained. "But I was outside talking to the lady next door and when I went back into the house I took one look at those guys and knew that something was wrong. Both of them are really the macho type, but they were pale and their eyes bugged out. They asked me, 'What was that music?' I asked them what they were talking about and they told me they'd heard chamber music coming from somewhere inside the house. I told them that was impossible since the power hadn't even been turned on, and there was no radio to explain what they'd heard."

The Petersens were so spooked by the house that they limited their visits to daylight hours and Frances gave up her plan to write a thesis there. But other odd things continued to occur.

"Once we took the old stove out of the attic and put it in the back of our car," Judith recalled. "The traffic was quite heavy that day and I breathed a quick prayer that we'd be safe on our return to Missoula. No sooner had I finished when a car rear-ended us. Thankfully, my son James was calm enough to step on the gas and get us out of the path of more traffic and the stove absorbed much of the shock, so nobody was hurt."

After that, the Petersens' cars often succumbed to a mysterious case of vapor lock on the way to Philipsburg. "I made twenty-some trips there and on five different occasions the cars just quit running around Drummond," James explained. "And that was with three different vehicles, so I couldn't figure out what was going on."

At those times when they were able to make it to Philipsburg, the Petersens experienced more spooky occurrences in what they'd once considered their dream house. One day Frances was coming down the stairs and she saw her mother sitting in a chair. "For a few seconds she looked like a totally different person, like an old woman wearing a shawl," Frances recalled. "It was almost as if the features of someone else had been superimposed on her."

Another time James was sleeping on the couch and woke up to see what may have been the same old woman standing on the stairs. "She had gray hair, was probably about five feet tall, and I'd guess she weighed between eighty and ninety pounds," he remembered. "I let out a holler and looked away for a second, and when I looked back she was gone. But she looked just like a real person. There was nothing hazy or misty about her."

The family members were so disturbed by the strange events that they asked a priest from Missoula to come to the house to say a mass. He prayed for the soul of the woman who was haunting the residence and he also entreated her not to bother the Petersens anymore. While the priest was still in the house, Judith was coming down the stairs and almost stepped on a marble that seemed to have appeared from nowhere.

"We had just cleaned that house, paying special attention to the stairs, so I have no idea where the marble came from," she said. "It looked like an old-fashioned one made of clay. If I hadn't seen it in time, I'm sure I would have stepped on it and fallen down the stairs. Then there might have been two lady ghosts haunting the house."

The Petersens learned that past owners had also had strange experiences there. "I was a real estate broker and one day I was talking to a fellow at the courthouse about the title to the property," Judith said. "He didn't elaborate, but he told me, 'I lived there once, and that was the unluckiest time of my whole life.'"

Judith recalls another former owner from California who stopped by during a visit to her grandparents. "She came into the back door of the kitchen and while she was talking to me she kept looking at the place where the kitchen stairs had gone up to the back room. In years past, probably after the woman fell to her death, the opening to the stairs had been blocked off and a closet was put over it. But this former owner kept looking at that part of the room. I asked her how it felt to come back to Philipsburg and she just said, 'I didn't leave anything here.' I thought that was an odd remark and I noticed that she seemed glad to get out of the kitchen as soon as she could.

"Another time two workmen came to turn on the heat or something and it was clear that they felt funny about going down into the basement," Judith said. "The job didn't take both of them, but it was clear that neither one would have gone down there by himself."

When the Petersens rented the house as they had originally intended to do, two different sets of tenants claimed that their children had nightmares whenever they slept in the back bedroom upstairs. The kids woke up screaming, but as soon as they were moved into another room they had no problems sleeping through the night.

Eventually the Petersens got tired of the house in Philipsburg and sold it to a dentist, who eventually sold it himself. "I don't know who lives there now, but you couldn't pay me enough to set foot in that place again, even after all these years," Frances insisted.

And yet it seems that no one who has lived in the house after the Petersens has reported any unusual occurrences, according to Philipsburg newspaper publisher Trilby Neitz who did some checking around for me. I also tried to get more historical information about the house, but I learned nothing that shed light on the strange documents the Petersens discovered in the attic.

I spoke with the Petersens' former neighbor, Dolly Page, and with Leonard Bowen, grandson of William Bowen who, along with his brother Fred, built the Petersens' house and the one next to it. The brothers built the houses so that they were mirror images of each other and an unsubstantiated rumor is that there was originally a tunnel running between the two structures. The Petersens owned the house that belonged to William, and their neighbor Dolly Page lived in the one that William's brother Fred owned.

Dolly lived in her house for thirty-two years and she told me that she was unaware of ghost stories involving either of the two places, although she remembers the Petersens telling her about their experiences. Neither she nor Leonard Bowen has any idea who the mysterious woman who reportedly fell down the stairs might have been and neither knows of any boarders taken into the houses by members of the Bowen family. Dolly remembers that two Bowen daughters lived in the Petersens' house for a number of years, but she doesn't recall hearing that either of them was injured in a fall.

As far as Leonard Bowen knows, no elderly woman lived in the house during the time described in the letter. His grandmother was a young woman with a five-year-old child when she died in 1894 and Leonard doesn't believe that any other woman was living in the house then. And he knows of no one in the family who was a concert pianist, although he says that nearly all his relatives played music, especially his father's sister Lottie.

Of course, it's possible that the Petersens were mistaken about the dates of the events referred to in the mysterious letter. Those things might have happened to later inhabitants of the house after the Bowen family had left. It's even possible that the letter and the hearse receipt could have described events taking place somewhere else. One especially puzzling question is why the letter informing someone of the woman's death should be found in the house from which it was supposedly mailed. The Petersens believe that the letter they found was an original instead of a copy, so this might be an important consideration.

The mystery of the old house in Philipsburg gets deeper and deeper the more one delves into it. But as far as the Petersens are concerned, they had all of it they could stand—of its ghosts, its unearthly music, and its crotchety old woman who fell (or was she pushed?) down the stairs.

# Eleven

# "The Ghastly Form with Silent Tread"

O ne of the most spine-tingling ghost stories in Montana had its origins in a brutal murder that took place over one hundred and twenty years ago in a lonely tavern on the stage road between Helena and Deer Lodge. In the 1860s, this small hotel was owned by a hardworking Frenchwoman and her drunken lout of a husband, who spent so much of each day sampling the beers, wines, and whiskeys in his own bar that he had no time or energy to take care of his customers. Thus it was his industrious wife who cooked all the meals, took care of the guests, and did all the other chores to keep the tavern running.

Many of the clientele were miners who paid for their room and board with gold dust that the Frenchwoman wisely concealed from the eyes of her wasteful husband. One day when she thought he was away she brought out her secret savings, only to be surprised by his sudden return.

As the man stood looking at his wife's carefully accumulated treasure, rage and greed destroyed whatever was left of good in him. He killed his wife, took her gold dust, and disappeared. The poor Frenchwoman who had worked so hard to earn a living for herself and her husband was buried in the backyard of the tavern, which passed on to new owners.

Over the years, guests of the tavern claimed that the woman's spirit had never left the place where her unhappy life ended so cruelly. And on June 18, 1923, the *Dillon Examiner* published the hair-raising tale of Dr. C. S. Whitford of Butte, son of a famous Montana pioneer who had also been a physician. The younger Dr. Whitford claimed to have encountered the Frenchwoman's ghost on a visit to the old tavern in 1877 and a caption underneath his picture explains that he was offering his story forty-six years later "as an addition to discussions of spiritism evoked by preachments of Sir Arthur Conan Doyle on his visit to the United States."

Conan Doyle, the creator of the fictional detective Sherlock Holmes, was himself a fervent believer that the dead could communicate with the living. In fact, his later years were spent largely in writing and lecturing on the subject, but it is doubtful that even such a master of suspense as he could have written an account of a supernatural experience more riveting than Whitford's. Because the tale is so compelling in its details and so charming in its typical language of the period, I have excerpted large portions of it as follows:

He who travels over the lonely and deserted grounds of a once wild and exciting mining country travels over many mysteries, dark secrets, and bloody deeds of murder, robbery, and rapine, and the only witnesses were the grim and frowning mountains in whose dark shadows they were enacted. Hidden in some lonely nook many an unmarked and forgotten grave may yet be seen, within whose clammy, mildewed walls some unfortunate has slept these many years, and whose only crime was that of being near the murderous hand and heart that coveted his victim's gold.

What on earth speaks louder of loneliness than an unknown single grave lying within a little defile of the mountains, without a tree or spring to enliven the desolate aspect of the scene.

One wet, cold and stormy evening in the fall of 1877, my chum, John Vial and myself were slowly but thankfully nearing on heavy, muddy roads, and with jaded horses, an old, dilapidated and abandoned stage station nestled serenely and solitary among the Dog Creek mountains midway between Deer Lodge and Helena, our stopping place for the night.

We were met pleasantly by a man who eyed us with (I am sure) feeling of pity for our wet and half-frozen condition, and bidding us walk into the house, soon had our miserable horses detached from the vehicle and comfortably stalled and fed in the stable, which, from casual observation, looked much more cozy than the house, the latter, exteriorly considered, being a long, one-story log structure, rough, dirty and moldy, presenting an abode about as cheerless as a discouraged and worn-out traveler could well imagine. The dwelling was rudely composed of each extreme end, kitchen in the rear, with large rooms in the center, into which we were ushered and, save for a large old fireplace, on which the flames were rising warm and bright, the interior would have presented as cold and cheerless a picture as the outside.

In due time we found ourselves quite dry and comfortable and made happy and satisfied as we lingered over a plentiful and delicious supper, after which we lighted our pipes and sat around the mammoth fireplace. We chatted pleasantly with the proprietor. Mines, farms, stock interests and various other subjects were discussed until we became fairly talked out, when our cold, benumbed nerves succumbed to the genial aspects of the warm, blazing fire, and we (I, for one at least) silently sat, dreamily watching the pictures of my life as they passed to and fro through the camera of the coals. Whoever has indulged in pleasant phantasies and delightful dreams that did not suffer an abrupt awakening, to be plunged into some mental or physical agony? Thus it proved to me soon after.

We were allotted as our sleeping apartment the little bedroom in the west end of the building, and being shown the way by the proprietor, he gave us a light and bade us good night. After securely fastening the door and window and, while preparing for bed, we observed that we occupied an ordinary room about 12 feet square, containing a double bed, an old organ, chairs and a small bureau over which hung a glass, at the foot of the bed. Raising the window blind sufficiently to allow the rays of the moon to light up the objects about us, we extinguished the sallow glim of the candle and lay down to slumber. Weary bones took kindly to the soft and downy influence of sheets and pillows, and sleep soon transported me to the land of dreams, where the brain might take respite in the fields of the unknown.

## An Apparition

I had not slept long before some unaccountable influence caused me to suddenly awake and sit bolt upright, staring at the hazy and dimly-outlined figure and form of a woman slowly advancing with outstretched arms toward the bed. My endeavor to arouse my companion seemed an age, and when accomplished, the apparition had receded to the shadowed corner of the room opposite our position, and three times slowly extending her right arm towards us, she vanished within the space from whence she came. You will, no doubt, exclaim: "There is nothing remarkable in such a demonstration," and so should I (then) and this story never would have been written but for what followed. Had the strange occurrence ceased at this point I would have gladly and for all time charged it to the imagination of a disordered mind. Sleep, of course, forsook me; not so my companion, who, having seen nothing unnatural, and immediately recovering from the fright of my having assured him that I had, soon slumbered again, much to my contempt and disgust. Nothing but the heavy slumber of my partner broke the awful stillness of the tomb-like place, when an hour and a half of fearful suspense had passed, my eyes were again staring at the sight of the same ghastly form of the woman once more appearing at the same corner. I awakened my companion again, who saw nothing, and I vainly pointed out the spectre. I described to him minutely her movements, which were perceptibly bold, this time proceeding a few feet farther from the corner to the old organ where she disturbed the papers lying thereon, taking the while a paper scroll in her left hand, and again making three ominous gestures with her right, disappeared as noiselessly as before.

You may well imagine that I was thoroughly awake and quite astonished at the uncanny visitation of the dead in such form. My sleepy companion, seeing nothing all this time, was simply nervous over my actions—saying repeatedly, "Imagination! Imagination!"

I endeavored to make myself believe that I was the victim of some hallucination, but impossible the spirit form of a human being had plainly appeared twice in its weird and ghastly lineaments.

As I was not then a believer in the occult, I resolved to keep the secret of the vision and to impress the necessity of secrecy on my companion if possible, so that if it was an hallucination we would not be ridiculed for having seriously mentioned it. How eagerly I wished the morning, the noise and motion of day to change this terrible scene at night. At last the glorious light of dawn appeared, finding me excited and busy with my thoughts, my companion sleeping heavily by my side. I began to feel as though some evil influence had been shaken from me and all the heavy oppressiveness of the night gone, and in its place a relaxed and exhausted sensation, and my eyelids closed in sleep once more.

## Third Visitation

Again suddenly and mysteriously awakened, while the light of day flooded the room, rendering all objects clearly discernible, comes for the third time into my horrified vision the ghastly form with silent tread. With what little strength I still possessed I drew myself to a sitting posture, while my hair fairly stood on end, breathlessly I watched its movements. I remember seeing a tall form covered with a long white shadowy shroud with an indefinable, delicate mist surrounding it; raven-black hair hanging in loose tresses down the back; face snowy white, narrow and pinched, with an indescribable expression of pain and sorrow in features only, as the eyes were represented by large, dark and shadowy caverns whose depths seemed fathomless. My companion looked at me as though I were bereft of my senses, earnestly assuring me I must be suffering from the effects of a dream, for he could see nothing to be alarmed at. Every silent action of her unearthly form did I eagerly watch, while the cold perspiration gathered in huge drops on my body, when she quickly swept to the foot of the bed, brushed her hair back with her hand, while peering into the looking glass, then finally turned and, leaning far over the foot board and looking me full in the face, turned me rigid and speechless. What torture I endured in that terrible moment, wildly, almost insensibly staring at that unnatural and ghastly form of death, no one can imagine. She came without sound to the side of the bed and slowly bending over my companion, placed her deathly hand upon my head. I shall forever see that agonized sorrow-stricken countenance appearing as though she would speak and disclose some secret.

My companion laboriously chafed my hands and face. The warm bright sunshine lighting up our room, every vestige of the wierd [*sic*] scenes of the night seemed to have vanished.

While Dr. Whitford's weird scenes of night vanished with the coming of day, we can be sure that the memory of those scenes never faded with time. And even today, nearly seventy years after the doctor revealed the tale of his uncanny visitation by the dead, who among us would dare to spend a night so close to the grave of the poor, murdered Frenchwoman?

# Twelve

## Accompanied by Angels

Those who believe that encounters with the supernatural are intrinsically evil and frightening might think differently after hearing the beautiful story told so often to Bert Ewell by his mother.

"To the best of my knowledge, she never told a lie in her life," Bert said. "And although I heard the tale repeated many times over the years, the details were always essentially the same."

The incidents of the story to which he refers occurred some sixty years ago when Bert was five or six years old and living in Lewistown, Montana. "We were quite poor at the time, since we had a large family and a limited income," he recalled. "But most of our friends were in the same financial circumstances and neighbors were glad to help each other out whenever they could."

On one occasion the mother of a dying child asked Bert's mother and several other women to sit with her at her daughter's bedside. As the little girl's suffering grew worse, the watchers got down on their knees to pray.

"Suddenly, a bright glow appeared in one corner of the room, up at the ceiling," Bert said. "And as everyone looked on in amazement, something which appeared to be the life force of the little girl arose from the body on the bed and floated just above the heads of the women. Two or three small angel-like beings accompanied the child's soul as it rose up and finally disappeared through the wall."

The women then turned to look at the still form on the bed. "Mom told me that the little girl had the most peaceful expression on her face," Bert remembered, "a kind of smile, as though she were no longer in pain and had nothing more to fear."

Bert, who still lives in Lewistown, doesn't remember the names of the other people involved in the tale, and the little house on the alley on Daws Street where the incident occurred is no longer there. But the story itself, providing such a reassuring glimpse of what lies beyond our earthly lives, will always remain with him, as it surely will with anyone else fortunate enough to hear it.

# Thirteen

## "Hoodoos" at the Butte-Silver Bow County Courthouse

When you consider all the real-life dramas played out every day in the nation's courthouses and jails, and if you accept the theory that hauntings arise from highly charged emotions that somehow become imprinted on their physical environment, you won't be surprised to learn that the Butte-Silver Bow County Courthouse has a stray spook or two.

On Halloween 1991, the *Montana Standard* ran a front page story by Peter Chapin with the headline "Workers say ghost haunts courthouse." As if he appreciated the publicity, that very evening the same ghost appeared again to Gene Griffith, a night watchman whose various encounters with the apparition had been featured in the article. In addition to actually having seen the ghost, Gene and several other employees had been plagued by such things as phantom footsteps, doors opening and closing by themselves, and an elevator with a mind of its own.

But before we discuss the weird things that are still happening at the Butte-Silver Bow County Courthouse, it may be helpful to look at the history of the site. The current courthouse was constructed in 1910 at the same spot as an earlier one and the locale has been the scene of well-documented psychic phenomena for many decades.

Back on October 17, 1909, the *Butte Miner* published an article that may shed light on what's going on at the courthouse even now. Author Charles F. Degelman posed the central question in his headline: "Is Murderer's Ghost Haunting the Butte County Jail?" A subheading is equally intriguing: "Object in Human Form Supposed to be Jail Yard Intruder Vanishes in Air Before Eyes of Officers. No Accounting for Spooky Occurrence—the Spirit Hovers Around Gruesome Relics." To the right of this subheading is another: "Deputy Sheriffs and Others Cannot Be Shaken From Belief That They Have Frequently Seen Spirit Form of Miles Fuller, Who Was Hanged Here Several Years Ago for Cruel Murder."

The Butte–Silver Bow County Courthouse, where psychic phenomena have been reported for decades. (*Photograph courtesy Walter Hinick*)

The article goes on to detail the numerous uncanny incidents that had been occurring for some time, many of them taking place in or near the rear portion of the building under the county jail. Degelman explains that the stories had recently become so persistent and had been "vouched for by so many practical and hard-headed men who were not at all likely to be deceived or to be the victims of a superstitious fear, that [the newspaper] detailed one of its local representatives to investigate the matter, and the results are truly startling."

Startling indeed, for the story that follows is as riveting as anything written by Stephen King, with the added bonus that everything in it was reported as the truth by those involved.

A number of the witnesses hesitated to describe what they had seen as "visible manifestations of disembodied spirits," but they also "unhesitatingly declared that they could not account for those manifestations on the basis that they were produced by living persons in a spirit of fun or for any other motive that might be imagined." Several deputy sheriffs insisted that they had seen a person in the jailyard, conducted a search, but found no one—in spite of the fact that they realized no living person could have escaped without detection.

Most of the observers got a good look at the intruder and their description of him tallied exactly with that of Miles Fuller, "the aged gambler and prospector, as he appeared just before he met a violent death by hanging on the scaffold in the county jailyard." Fuller had been executed approximately three years earlier at 5:00 A.M. on May 18, 1906. His crime was killing fellow prospector Henry Gallahan, whom Fuller accused of interfering with some of his mining operations. Fuller had made threats to Gallahan before and the police immediately suspected him of the murder. They were able to track him to his cabin by some peculiar nail marks made by his shoes on the ground. But even though the evidence against Fuller was overwhelming, he never admitted that he was Gallahan's killer.

Some strange circumstances accompanied the condemned man's execution, with the result that some who were "inclined to be superstitious" predicted that if there were such things as ghosts, Fuller would definitely become one and return to seek vengeance on those responsible for his death.

One of these weird happenings occurred after Fuller's body was removed from the scaffold and placed in a coffin. So many people had a superstitious dread of being a pallbearer to a murderer that it was difficult to round up enough men to serve in that capacity. Eventually, however, six were found, and their duty was to load the casket onto a vehicle to take it to the undertaker.

"The weather that morning was not very clear," Degelman writes, "though thunder was not necessarily to be expected, but just as the coffin was about to be placed on the wagon preparatory to the trip to the last resting place for the mortal remains of the murderer, a heavy crash came.

"The occurrence was so startling at such a moment that it was only with considerable exertion of will power that the pall bearers retained their hold on the coffin," Degelman continues. "The clap of thunder was the only one of the morning. Of course, no rational person will for a moment believe that the occurrence was anything more than a coincidence, and . . . the persons who declare they have beheld the strange, ghostly appearances, declare emphatically to a man that they were not in the least degree influenced by any such stories that were told them, and in fact, most of them had not heard of those weird alleged premonitions of spirit visitations before they had the startling experiences they relate."

After Fuller's burial, his apparition was sighted in various parts of the jailyard, including the exact spot where his scaffold had stood. But his most usual haunt was a room lived in by several deputy sheriffs on the force of Sheriff O'Rourke. This room was located on the ground floor of the county jail building and it opened onto the courtyard, thirty feet from the site of the scaffold. All of the deputies living in the room had had experiences that initially made them suspect that a practical joker was at work. But, Degelman writes, "as soon as they made certain by investigation that the appearances they saw were not produced by any human means, they were free to admit and declare they could not account for the occurrences except on the theory that they had actually beheld a ghost or some supernatural manifestation."

But, except for the purpose of scaring the men when they were probably at their most vulnerable, why would the ghost appear in the deputies' living quarters? The most plausible explanation was that a scrapbook of "gruesome relics" from Fuller's hanging was kept in this room and a picture of two of the relics, an invitation to the hanging itself and a portion of the black cap that was pulled over the condemned man's face just before the trap was sprung, appears with the article. (Unfortunately, no one now knows the whereabouts of either the relics or the original photographs from the article.) The picture caption explains that the "somber-hued piece of cloth, it is believed, is an especial object of attraction to the ghost which has been seen as if wearing the cap with that portion of it missing."

Deputy Sheriff Tom Mulcahy had been given the grim souvenirs by deputies under ex-sheriff J. J. Quinn, in whose administration the hanging took place. Mulcahy believed that the ghost was attracted not so much by the scrap from the execution cap as by the photograph of Fuller that appeared on the invitation to his hanging. At first, Degelman writes, Mulcahy was pleased to have the relics, which also included a piece of the rope that hanged Fuller. But several nocturnal visits by the ghost of the hanged man had lessened his joy in possessing them. Only the fear of being made fun of by fellow officers kept him from throwing the things away when the weird events began and Degelman playfully adds that Mulcahy would not "admit that he has any desire that the ghost that has been greatly troubling his slumbers in that room should take the relics away with it on the next trip, if it is so inclined."

In several interviews regarding the strange phenomena, Mulcahy insisted that repeated visits by the ghost had somewhat reduced his fear and he was determined to keep the relics after all. "I don't believe Fuller is able to take them away in the shape he is in now," Mulcahy is quoted as saying. "If that is really his ghost that I have seen in that room 25 times or more, . . . I believe I will be able to hold on to the things all right. I would not like to have anybody steal them and then try to make me believe the spirit got them. If anybody did get them, he might be sorry for it afterwards, although it would remain to be seen whether Fuller would go out of that jail yard to hunt them up."

The deputy sheriff had become increasingly irritated when anyone doubted his sincerity about the phantom encounters. To his detractors he was reported to have said on several occasions, "Well, all right, if you think I am kidding I have nothing more to say except that there is a bed that is not in use now in that room. You can sleep in it for awhile and see for yourself. I warrant you will be scared out the same as several other fellows were who took up the dare, who were just as skeptical as you are when I told them about it."

And then Mulcahy describes the terrifying events that had driven him and so many other men from that room. Large portions of his story are excerpted below:

> The thing appeared to me first just like it was coming in a window in a sort of foggy, dim light. I let out a yell and jumped up as quick as I could and turned on the light. Fritz Hugo, the other deputy who was sleeping in the room with me at the time, is a sound sleeper. My yell woke him up all right, but before he got his eyes open and was sitting up in bed I had the light turned on and there was nothing more to be seen. Hugo goes to sleep as soon as he hits the pillow and he says he has never seen anything, but he admits that he has on several occasions felt something just like a breeze passing over his face and the bedclothes being pulled down at times when a strange racket would awaken him in that room. I know he suspected me of having pulled the bedclothes off him and caused a breeze to go over his face, but I am sure he has gotten over that idea long ago because the same things happened a number of times when he knew that I was not around and nobody else was in the room to disturb him.

> I never had any experience with ghosts before, if that is what you call the experience I had in that room, and I do not think I can be called a man who is in any way inclined to be superstitious or easily taken in with any such thing, but what I see and comes plainly before my eyes, I see, and that is all there is about it. Another man who had the

same experience I had, and who was also scared, and who let out a yell when he first saw the thing was Mike Friel [the name is also spelled "Freil" elsewhere in the story]. The poor fellow is dead now, and is not here to tell his experiences himself. He was accidentally killed last week on the flats while duck hunting. Mike had enough bad luck and some people who are superstitious, as they claim now I am, might be inclined to imagine that Fuller's ghost followed him and hoodooed him in some way. He was as fine a fellow as anybody would ever want to meet, but he lost his position as a deputy sheriff through a foolish scrape that nobody would ever imagine so sensible a fellow would get into, and the next thing he goes down on the flats and gets in front of a loaded shotgun just as it is being fired at a duck, and is killed.

Even if I do claim that I saw something that must have been the ghost of Miles Fuller on more occasions than I can count, I still say I am not superstitious as I have said a number of times before. I am not afraid to stay in that room, and I do not intend to give up any of those relics for fear that some sort of hoodoo will overtake me as seemed to have overtaken poor Mike Freil. As I said before, his getting into a silly scrape that lost him his position on the sheriff's force seemed unaccountable on the part of so sensible a fellow, and I understand that he was always considered a very level headed and careful fellow on hunting trips, and how it was that he became so careless as to step in front of that loaded gun is almost as unaccountable as the other proposition.

I have been asked about that but I do not understand why Fuller should have had a grudge against Mike any more than against me, for neither of us had any connection with the hanging, except that I saw it. I recall, however, that once Freil let out a terrible oath when he was disturbed by the thing and grabbed a pistol just as I turned on the light again. I believe he would have shot at it if the thing had not disappeared too quickly for him to get in action with his gun. Several times after that when Mike was out and I was alone when the thing appeared, I saw it give a very ugly look in the direction of Mike's empty bed just before it seemed to float out of the window and disappear again.

I believe it is not right to recall bad traits even of a dead murderer who has paid the terrible penalty for his crime, but in order to make a point that I am thinking of I must say that Fuller while alive, had a fearfully ugly and malicious disposition. He laid for that poor man, and not only shot and killed him, but also ran up and cut his throat with a big knife after he must have been almost dead from the gunshot wound, and no doubt some people might say who were inclined to be superstitious in that way, which I claim I am not, that Fuller's spirit is just as ugly and malicious now as he was in life, and that his spirit might have had something to do with bringing about the misfortunes of poor Mike Freil before he died and his violent taking off.

Some of my friends are trying to make me believe now that I am under a hoodoo and that I had better quit that room or I will loose [sic] my job or get killed or something like that, but, of course, that is all a josh, they are just kidding me. I will stay with the room and when I take a notion I will go duck hunting, too. In regard to what I see, it is not easy to describe the appearance minutely, for it usually comes just like a flash, and, although I have got somewhat used to it, I am a little nervous and excited yet whenever I see it. I do not jump up and yell as I did at first, and I believe I have had a better view of it lately than I ever did before. There are always the same long gray whiskers like Fuller wore, and once in a good light I was certain that I saw objects like a black cap on his head and a piece of rope dangling.

Of course, it is foolish to think a person can harm a ghost or affect it in any way by shooting at it, but I was bewildered and excited the first few times it appeared and I grabbed my gun quick, as a man will when he is excited if he has a gun handy, as I always have in my business. I was never afraid of old man Fuller when he was alive and I guess I have less reason to be afraid of him now that he is dead, but just the same I had my revolver in my hand when I jumped out of bed and turned on that light. As I said before, the gray beard was always in sight. It seemed like it was showing through a hole in the bottom of the black cap, and it flashed across my mind one night when he was poking around in a bureau drawer where I kept it, that he was trying to find the piece of cap I had to patch up that hole with.

I keep Fuller's photograph in a scrap book, where I have a lot of the horse dope from the time when I was in the racing business, and riding in England and France and this country. I have a whole lot of newspaper clippings about myself in that book, and I would not lose it for a farm. One night when I thought I heard the drawer being opened in which I kept that scrap book, I jumped up and turned on the light, and sure enough that drawer was standing open. I was not certain but what the drawer had been left open by some of us, but Mike Freil claimed it was closed when he went to bed. Before I could get the light turned on something like what I had often seen before appeared to vanish in the direction of that window. I took the book then and put it under my pillow, and what do you think of that? I felt something tugging at that book under my head not a minute after I laid [sic] down again, and it seemed to me that if I had not grabbed hold of it, that book would have been gone.

I have never paid much attention to such things and do not know what people claim spooks are capable of doing, but I believe they have never been accused of taking anything away. That scrapbook has been in that bureau drawer all the time since, and I have never been able to tell from any change in its position that it was ever disturbed. Some of the boys were kidding Fritz Hugo and me not long ago because a lot of our clothes were missing one night. I knew right away that some live ghost had been to work, and I went out into the driveway in the jailyard and found a black derby hat that would have been two or three sizes too large for Fuller. I knew then that there had been a burglar around, and did some gumshoe work as fast as I could to get our clothes back again. I had a fellow named Charles Clark, who had just finished a term in jail, and who had done some work as a trusty, under suspicion right away.

I found Clark, and the hat was a perfect fit for him. He almost as much as admitted that he had been disturbed in his job and lost the [derby] in making his getaway in a hurry. I also found some pawn tickets and rescued the clothes from a hock joint. Clark is still in jail awaiting trial on a burglary charge. I never said much about the incident before because we were ashamed of having it get out that a burglar had broken into the room of two deputy sheriffs right in the jail building and swiped a lot of our clothes. When some of the boys were joshing me about Fuller having taken our stuff, I said I did not believe the ghost could carry away anything, and I showed them a big hole in the wire screen in the window. I said if it had been Fuller he would not have made that hole in the screen as he had always come and gone through that window glass, screen and all, without any trouble. Then the boys said his ghost might have been able to get through that way itself, but it had to make a hole in the screen in order to get the clothes through with it. I suppose some people will think that losing our clothes was a part of the bad luck that came to us through that hoodoo spook.

In regard to other persons who had some experience in that room I will mention two incidents. One man made me swear that I would never mention his name, as his experience was so startling and spooky and he said his wife and children would be scared to death of him if they knew he had had a wrestling match with a ghost. The fellow started in very bravely and was tucked in under the covers very nicely when I left the room to go up town for a while. I asked if he wanted the light turned out. He said "Certainly," and I turned it out. When I returned in about 20 minutes Mr. Bravefollow [sic] was sitting up in a chair near the bed with part of his clothes on and getting the rest of them on as fast as he could. He swore that he had had all of that ghost he wanted and was going home. He said he locked the door after I went out to make certain that no one would come in to play pranks on him without his knowledge. He had just laid [sic] down again when something grabbed him around the neck and he could feel something like a piece of cloth and piece of rope dangling about his face.

He let out a yell and got up and turned on the light and made certain that there was no one else in the room and that neither the door nor the window and the screen had been disturbed and then he began preparations to dig out of there. He did not want to stay even after I returned and he said I was a fool for staying in such a place. I had never told the fellow that I had seen the thing with a cap on its head and a piece of rope dangling, but it seems that he felt them as well as myself seeing them. Now what do you think of that experience?

I have a friend named Fred Gallagher who is as fine and sensible a fellow as you would wish to meet and one of the best mixologists in the state. He got very brave too one night and went to bed in that room to see what he could see. I left him in bed and responded to a call to go down on the flats. It was reported that a drunken man there was torturing two horses. When I returned the room was empty; my friend was gone. I thought something had happened to induce the man to leave a room in the middle of the night after he had taken off all his clothes and gone to bed. When I met him again he did not have so much to say as the other fellow had, but I will leave it to anybody that something must have happened in the hour . . . that I was gone to cause a man to get out of bed and dress and go to another room at that time of night.

Later in the same article, Gallagher himself gives his own version of the evening's events, prefacing it by claiming to be "afraid of live people more than I am of dead ones." Gallagher left the room, he said, not because he was afraid of any ghost, but because he didn't like "the way Tom Mulcahy got to dancing aroun [sic] there reckless with a pistol in his hands." For that reason, and not a supernatural one, Gallagher insists, he had decided to leave the room before Mulcahy returned from the flats. "I knew he would not hurt the ghost any with his gun but I was not so certain that he might not do me some harm," Gallagher explains. Then he adds, "I have warned Tom several times that he has given me too much notoriety by telling around town what he says happened to me that night, and if he does not quit it some day he will run across something that will do more damage to him than a ghost. I got all I wanted of it that time, and I want to go out of the spook business entirely."

If Gallagher was a complete skeptic on the subject of the ghost, Deputy Fritz Hugo was not, although he too thought that human trickery might possibly have been involved in the strange occurrences. His account follows:

> I was awakened a number of times by the yells of Tom Mulcahy as he would jump out of bed and turn on the light. By that time there was nothing to be seen. I suppose; at least I did not see anything, and Mulcahy always said the spook was gone then. I must admit there were things I could not account for going on around there besides his yelling. Before the light went on I could feel something like a breeze going across my face and the bedclothes being pulled off me. I suspected that Tom or Mike Friel had something to do with that, but I could not understand how they could possibly have worked it under the conditions and I would have been fighting mad if I had found out they were playing such tricks on me. I do not believe in any hoodoos, and what happened to poor Mike Friel will not keep me from going duck hunting some time this fall if I take a notion to go. I will not go where he went simply because I do not believe there are any ducks around there to amount to anything, but I will go somewhere else.

Fuller's specter was clearly causing a lot of trouble, both to those who believed in him and those who did not. Besides making visits to the bedsides of the deputies, he also reportedly appeared one night in the jailyard, precipitating a search by officers who initially believed themselves to be chasing a live person. Details of the incident were related by Dan J. McCarthy, described as "one of the most practical and matter of fact deputies on Sheriff O'Rourke's force":

> Late one night several months ago, . . . the alarm was raised by Henry Woodthorpe, one of the courthouse janitors who was working in the rear of the place, that he had seen a man prowling around in the jailyard. Three or four of us deputies were in the office at the time, and we rushed out there to capture the fellow. We did not think anything about the ghost story, as I had not paid any attention to it, and I believe Woodthorpe was not mixed up in it either. There were some desperate prisoners in the jail at the time, and our idea was as we rushed out there that somebody was prowling around in an attempt to give some of the prisoners a chance to escape. Sometimes, too, dope is passed through some of the lower windows in the woman's [sic] department. We posted a man in the hallway to prevent an escape that way, and we knew

that a man who was in that backyard could not possibly got [*sic*] away from us, as at that time the high and solid brick wall around the jailyard which has since been demolished partially on account of the operations in connection with the building of the new jail, was still standing. The wall had broken glass all over the top and there were no ladders around that would have given a man a chance to scale it in any sort of hurry. The way the thing happened, the janitor had scarcely lost sight of the object when we were on the scene searching for it.

Strange to tell, we searched thoroughly in every place in which a person could possible [*sic*] have secreted himself, and found not a trace of a human being. I am telling the thing just as it happened, and anybody else can draw his conclusions. The janitor said that the fellow he saw was an old man with whiskers, and then I was reminded of the Fuller ghost stories. I know the janitor was not fooling us, and he seemed terribly puzzled when we failed to find anyone around there and the jailyard gate was locked securely as we always kept it those times.

Janitor Henry Woodthorpe was also interviewed and described the sighting of the apparition that began the fruitless search. Woodthorpe was coming out of the boiler room under the jail and he was able to see clearly because of a dim light burning over his head. "I saw the man or whatever it was that was in the form of a man, as plainly as if it had been daylight, standing, I should judge, about twenty feet away," Woodthorpe is quoted as saying. "I was terribly surprised when the deputies and myself failed to find anybody around, and am certain no man could have made his escape over that high wall in the time he would have had to do it in. I do not know anything about ghosts, and if anybody can account for the occurrence he can do better than I can. I heard it was told around that I took a couple of shots at the form I saw, but that is not true. I never shoot at anything around the courthouse. It would be a very reckless and wrong thing to do."

The *Butte Miner* article ends at this point, but it is accompanied by a large inset detailing the facts surrounding Fuller's crime and execution, as well as a "metaphysical opinion" by a "prominent theosophist of Butte" who refused to divulge his name. According to the inset, the theosophist "declared emphatically that such occurrences as are described in the narrative here printed are as well authenticated as almost anything else in history of man's experiences on earth.

"It is held by many occult investigators that the spirit of a man who is suddenly taken away from life in a violent manner, remains for an indefinite period in a confused state," the inset continues. "It is often not able to entirely disassociate itself from the surroundings of its violent taking off, and seems to be attracted to objects directly connected with that taking off as with the piece of rope and black cap in connection with the Fuller hanging."

Could this classic explanation of what a haunting entails explain the strange events still taking place at the Butte–Silver Bow County Courthouse more than eighty-six years after the execution of Miles Fuller? If so, the intensity of the manifestations, if not the force of Fuller's rage, has diminished considerably over the years. This pattern seems to hold true in most hauntings that occur repeatedly over time, and many kinds of psychic phenomena eventually fade away completely. Does the diminishing effect occur because the troubled spirit finally finds peace, or because the energy imprinted on the environment weakens with time? The answer to this question, if it is ever found, will go a long way toward providing religious, ethical, and even scientific explanations of all paranormal phenomena.

But back to the courthouse and the recent ghostly occurrences there. At least one apparition has been seen several times by various employees, although it is unclear whether the specter is that of Miles Fuller. In fact, none of those who saw the ghost mentioned his having a beard and Fuller was known to have worn a long, gray one of the style popular at the time. One farfetched story is that the courthouse ghost is that of a headless miner, but I was unable to locate anyone who claimed to have seen a spook lacking any crucial body parts.

Payroll supervisor Rick Soto believes that the apparition he encountered almost three years ago was wearing clothing that indicated he was from an earlier time. "I was working late one evening and I believe that I was the only one in the building aside from the night watchman," he explained. "In the area where I work, the only way to get from one office to another is to walk completely through each one; there's no outside hallway to get you from one to the other. I was doing data entry on the work station in the very first office and out of the corner of my eye I saw somebody walk the entire way through all of the offices. I heard the person walking too, because as he was coming around the corner, he or she or whatever it was made a kind of rasping noise against the door frame.

"It startled me because I thought I was the only one there, so I got up to see who it was. I walked through all the offices toward where I had last seen the person, turning on all the lights as I went. But when I got through to the last office, I couldn't see anybody.

"Suddenly I had this strange sensation. I got goose pimples and the whole thing really bothered me," Rick admitted. "And another funny thing happened that night when I was leaving my office on the second floor. When I pressed the button for the elevator to come up from the first floor, the doors opened, but there was no elevator. There was just an empty shaft, pitch black. That really spooked me. I went down the stairs, doing a hundred miles an hour, just to get out of the building."

Rick recalled one coffee break some time after his experience when he heard other employees talking about how Miles Fuller's ghost still haunts the area between the courthouse and the jail building. "There's an underground tunnel that goes from one to the other now and they say he's been seen walking through it," Rick said. "They asked me what the person I saw looked like and I told them that he was wearing long boots, a long, light-colored canvas type of coat like miners used to wear, and a hat like old-time firemen wore."

If the ghost Rick saw isn't Fuller, who does he think it might be?

"One man I spoke with said that the original courthouse building burned at one time and during its reconstruction a man had an accident and was killed," Rick explains. "Some people think that it's his spirit who walks through the courthouse from time to time. I've only seen this person once, but now whenever I work at the courthouse after hours, I lock the main door to our office and put a garbage can in front of the door. That way, anyone who opens the door will knock down the trash can and I'll hear it."

Rick admits that he received a lot of ribbing from his coworkers when the *Montana Standard* ran its article describing his experience and those of other employees. "It's pretty interesting, though, that some of these same people I work with have admitted to me that they've met up with the ghost, although they would never go to the media or tell anyone else."

One of these other brave souls who wasn't afraid to share his ghost stories with the newspaper or with me is night watchman Gene Griffith, who has had more encounters with the courthouse ghost than anyone else in recent years. In fact, he has seen the apparition so many times since the first occasion in 1983 that he has come to view the spirit as a kind of friend, or at least a companion during his shift from 4:00 P.M. to midnight.

Once, at the end of August 1991, Gene encountered the ghost three times in one night. But, except for his first few meetings with the unearthly soul, Gene has never been particularly frightened, even when the apparition stared right back at him. "It's looked at me twice," Gene confessed, "and I could see right through the area of the head. I wasn't able to make out any facial features, but I could tell that it saw me, too."

Unlike Rick Soto, Gene believes that the ghost is from the 1950s or 1960s, since he seems to be wearing more modern clothing than that described by Rick. Gene claims to have come within a couple of feet of the six-foot-tall ghost, who wears old cavalry boots, an old cowboy's raincoat, and a wide-brimmed cowboy hat that usually covers most of his face.

Besides seeing the ghost, Gene has also heard doors opening and closing mysteriously and someone walking in the building when he knows it to be empty. And the most common phenomenon experienced by Gene, as well as by the other employees, is the strange behavior of the elevator.

When not in use, the elevator is supposed to be stationed at the first floor. "But it often goes by itself," Gene explained, "moving from floor to floor when no one is pushing the buttons. About once every six months it will do that. It will usually go from the first floor to the fourth and from the fourth to the basement, then back to the first."

Maintenance men say that they've repeatedly checked the mechanics of the elevator and there's no reason for it to take off by itself. The only reason it should move, and the only logical way that it can, is for someone inside it to press the buttons to direct it where to go.

On one occasion the elevator actually held a man and woman hostage. "My boss and his wife went to the courthouse for him to do some work," Rick Soto explained, "and they got into the elevator to take them to the second floor. The elevator immediately zoomed up to the fourth floor, and then my boss and his wife couldn't get the doors to open. The elevator went back to the basement and then it started going up and down, up and down, with them still in it. When they finally got it to stop, it did so between floors, so they still couldn't get out. They frantically pushed buttons to get it moving again, but this time it wouldn't budge. Then it started moving again, finally stopping once more between floors. This time, however, they were able to get out."

Another courthouse employee, unnamed in the *Montana Standard* article, said that the elevator once "yo-yoed" him among the floors until it let him loose in the basement. He hadn't planned to get off there, but as he didn't feel like arguing with any spooks, he left the elevator and dashed for the stairs.

Lights in the building have also been known to turn themselves on, according to Rick Soto. And Jerry Combo, a courthouse engineer who starts work at 4:00 A.M., admits that he's heard mysterious footsteps and doors opening and closing on their own, and he too has had to deal with the quirky elevator. But even though these things can't be explained, Jerry doesn't believe in phantoms. "Lots of crazy things happen in Butte, Montana," he says, "but they're not caused by ghosts."

Law librarian Joyce Bouchard is another skeptic who, nevertheless, has had experiences she can't figure out. She has seen books fall from the library shelves for no good reason and several times she has had the uneasy feeling of being watched in her workplace on the third floor. According to the *Montana Standard* article, those feelings were most prevalent about ten years ago, before the third floor was renovated and the mezzanine taken out.

Janitors Bill Ayers and Pat Maloughney have also experienced the eerie sensation of an unseen presence. "At times I've had the feeling that somebody was following me," Bill admitted. "On one night I must have turned around about a dozen times, because I had the feeling that someone was there." On another occasion, the two men were eating lunch when they heard doors opening and closing when no one else was around. And Bill, too, has heard the odd sounds of the elevator moving by itself.

Pat Maloughney hastens to explain that he really doesn't believe in ghosts, but he remembers hearing an elderly relative say that she witnessed a hanging behind the jail sometime during the 1920s. This was too late to be the execution of Miles Fuller, of course, but it seems plausible that any of the prisoners who were ever put to death on the grounds could be responsible for the manifestations that still occur.

The eerie phenomena affecting the courthouse and its employees are not limited to the buildings themselves. Officer Larry Malyevac remembers a cold night in January 1973 when he and his partner were working patrol duty for the Silver Bow County Sheriff's Department.

"We were in the south end of town about 3:00 A.M., driving west on Greenwood Avenue," Officer Malyevac recalled. "On the north side of Greenwood was a vacant lot and on the south side was Mount Mariah Cemetery. We were about one hundred yards west of Montana Street when my partner began slowing the car. I looked up and saw an older gentleman in a wheelchair. He was making his way from the vacant lot across the street in front of us and into the cemetery through a side gate.

"After the man in the wheelchair had gotten into the graveyard, my partner and I moved on," Officer Malyevac continued. "We drove about two blocks and my partner stopped the car again. I asked him what was wrong, because he had a funny look on his face. Finally he said, 'What's a guy in a wheelchair doing out here this time of night?'

"That did strike both of us as odd, so we turned the car around and drove back to the cemetery. And what we found was very unsettling. We'd both seen the man in the wheelchair go through the gate, but when we checked it, it was securely fastened with an old rusted padlock that looked as if it had been undisturbed for many years. Also, it was snowing that night and the only tracks in the street were those of our patrol car. There were absolutely no wheelchair tracks or marks of any other kind. And, obviously, we saw no trace of the mysterious man, either."

Officer Malyevac admitted that if he had been alone at the time of this experience, he would have decided that he had fallen asleep and dreamed the whole thing. "But my partner was driving and he was the first one to see the guy," he explained. He also insisted that the account could be verified by a cousin of his, Diane Nixon, who was working at a local truck stop that night and still remembers the two deputies telling her their story over steaming cups of coffee.

What are we to make of all the strange stories that have circulated around the Butte–Silver Bow County Courthouse for so many decades? Does the angry spirit of Miles Fuller still roam the site of his execution or has his ghost been replaced by more modern ones who have their own grievances against the courthouse and its employees? Or, since most of the recent hauntings seem more mischievous than menacing, could the current spook-in-residence be a friendly phantom just trying to relieve the loneliness of those who work the night shift? Amid all these questions, only one thing's for certain—when you're in the courthouse, you'd better take the stairs. The ghost will be using the elevator.

# Fourteen

## Some Ghosts Are Good Guys

**M**any people believe that, by definition, all ghost stories are frightening—that there's no way spooks can return from the great beyond without scaring the wits out of anybody unlucky enough to get in their way. Still other people confuse spirits of the dead with demons and, for that reason, believe that all supernatural manifestations are inherently evil. Those who have such prejudices against our spectral friends might decide to change their views after reading the following three stories about good and loving spirits who returned just long enough to comfort, reassure, and help the living.

The first account comes from Kathryn O'Connell of Helena, who had a very special relationship with her grandmother; as Kathryn herself describes it, the two were "connected," at times even communicating telepathically.

"When I was going to college, I'd often make plans with friends to see a movie or to go somewhere and at the last minute something would make me decide not to go," Kathryn explained. "Sometimes my friends got angry with me, saying that I was undependable. And inevitably, whenever that happened, the phone would ring and I knew even before picking it up that it was my grandmother calling, wondering if I wanted to go out with her.

"When she died, I was very sad, but I still felt her wonderful presence all around me," Kathryn recalled. "I remember going with the family to see her one last time before the funeral service. As I walked up to her casket, I thought how beautiful she looked lying there. Her body was dead, but I became aware somehow that her real being, her soul, had risen up, so that it was hovering just above and behind the coffin. And then, as plainly as if she were standing right next to me, I heard her laugh and say, 'Well, it's not as bad as I thought it would be!'

"I started to laugh too, and of course everyone around me thought that I'd lost my mind," Kathryn said. "Obviously, none of them heard what I did. But I was to have more contact with my grandmother in the days to come. For a long time after her funeral, I often woke up in my bedroom to see a golden globe, a ball of light, and I knew it was her spirit. I'm sure that I wasn't dreaming; in fact, the glowing sphere appeared so often in my room that finally I had to say, 'Grandma, I love you, but you can't stay here. You must go on.'

"That was two or three years ago, and I've never had the experience since then," Kathryn said. "I believe that after she died, she still wanted to be with me and to let me know that everything was all right on the other side."

Vicki Haakenson of Deer Lodge has a similar story about her grandfather, Dedric Madison Dyer, who lived in Vancouver, Washington, at the time of his death. Originally from eastern Tennessee, Madison, as everyone called him, had at one time driven the mail wagon from Butte to Dillon to Virginia City. His granddaughter describes him as "a big, big man, one of those wonderful people whom everybody loved."

Vicki was twelve years old when her grandfather died in April 1962, and until then, no one in her family had ever paid much attention to ghosts. "But just a day after he died, my family and I were sleeping in our little two-room house in Butte," she began. "It was quite an old place, with floors that creaked whenever anyone walked on them. My mother and stepfather slept in the front room on a hide-a-bed and we kids slept out on the back porch.

"My parents were suddenly awakened in the dead of night by footsteps clomping across the floor," she said. "These were heavy, loud steps made by a very large person, so my folks knew immediately that we kids weren't making the noise.

"Mom and Dad looked over to the doorway between the front room and the kitchen and they saw something misty and white filling the space, almost like a fog. They heard a voice talking, apparently to someone else that they couldn't see. Mom listened for a while, then whispered, 'I think it's Daddy.'

"By this time, even my skeptical stepfather was getting a little scared," Vicki said. "He sat up in bed and looked again at the doorway. Then he said, 'Madison!' And whatever had been there disappeared instantly. From that time on, my stepfather has believed in ghosts."

Vicki's memories of that night are just as vivid as those of her parents, because she too was visited by the kindly spirit. "I didn't hear him talking, but I woke up when he gently touched my shoulder and then sat down on the bed," she recalled. "At first I thought my little brother was sleepwalking and trying to climb into bed with me again, but then I opened one eye and saw a strange, foggy iridescence. I remember thinking, 'Well, this is a strange dream, but I feel as if Grandpa is here.' It was a very comforting experience, not frightening at all, so I just rolled over and went back to sleep.

"I discovered later that my sister had awakened to catch a glimpse of him too," Vicki continued. "But even more amazing was that on this very night my grandfather's spirit appeared to other family members in different locations."

Madison's children and grandchildren were scattered all over the western United States, Vicki explained, and only when the family members gathered for his funeral did they discover that he had made visits to each of them. "The evening after the services, all the relatives got together at one house and one of them mentioned having seen Grandpa. And then we all confessed that we'd had the same experience.

"Mom's youngest brother in Vancouver said that the spirit opened all the bedroom doors and then went in to check on everyone," Vicki said. "Grandpa went first into the children's room and then into the adults', where he nearly gave my uncle a heart attack. My aunt was frightened too, and crawled down to the foot of the bed to hide under the covers. Then the door shut again, but not before they heard Grandpa say to some unseen presence, 'Well, I'm ready to go home now. Let's go.' And then he left.

"He waited until the next night to visit my grandmother," Vicki said, "and he returned to her twice. So we all had contact with him after his death. This experience has made me realize that we don't actually lose people when they die and that there really is some kind of afterlife."

Parapsychologists record many instances of such visitations occurring just hours or days after someone has died (as well as at the exact moment of passing). One likely reason for psychic phenomena close to the time of death is that this is a transitional period for a soul leaving one world and entering the next. But ghosts are often known to manifest themselves years after their physical lives have ended. Consider, for example, what happened more than twenty years ago to Malcolm McDonald of Niarada, Montana.

Malcolm knew how to ride a horse by the time he was three or four years old and he usually enjoyed participating in cattle drives with the other members of his family. But on one drive when he was five or six, he became separated from his father and his older sister Lorrie. Malcolm was so young at the time that he now has trouble remembering all the details, but Lorrie, whose last name is now Meeks, has forgotten neither his getting lost nor the strange story he told afterward.

"Dad had always told Malcolm to stay on the trail, and if he got lost or frightened he was to give the horse its head so that it would go straight back to my Uncle Archie's house," she explained. "We all went off in different directions and later that afternoon when we rode down to meet each other we couldn't find Malcolm. We started to worry, so we rode on over to my uncle's house, where we found my little brother waiting for us. We just assumed that he had followed Dad's advice about allowing the horse to take him there and it wasn't until breakfast the next morning that we heard what had really happened.

"Malcolm said that he was riding down in the creek bottom where there was a lot of brush. He knew that bears had been spotted there and he got scared when he realized he was lost. But then, just as it started to get dark, a man on a horse came up to him and led him to Uncle Archie's place.

"My dad thought, naturally, that one of the neighbors must have helped Malcolm and he wondered which one it was. Malcolm described his rescuer as a tall man with very black hair. That ruled out one neighbor, who was bald. Then my brother said that the man who guided him to Uncle Archie's had had a mustache and very blue eyes. That description didn't fit anyone around Niarada, and none of us could figure out who Malcolm's good Samaritan might have been.

"Dad began asking him if the man was this person or that one and each time Malcolm said no. But he did remember that the mysterious man had ridden a 'pretty, pretty horse,' a big dapple-gray one. Nobody knew of anyone around Niarada who owned a horse like that, until Malcolm said, 'I remember something else, too. The horse's name was Gray Eagle.'

"As soon as he said that, my grandmother, in her late eighties at the time, looked very shocked. 'Tommy,' she said to my dad, 'that was your father's horse's name.'

"You can imagine how stunned we all were as we sat around the kitchen table that morning. And to this day," Lorrie added, "we're convinced that the man who guided Malcolm to Uncle Archie's house was the grandfather who died long before my brother was born. He was one of the early homesteaders; he was quite old, over sixty, when my father was born. He owned land for miles around and the original homestead was where Uncle Archie's ranch would be later. So it made perfect sense for my grandfather's spirit to be in that area and Malcolm's description of a tall man with black hair and blue eyes fit him perfectly.

"There's no way my brother could have known these things about his grandfather, because our grandmother almost never talked about him," Lorrie insisted. "And before that morning, she had never even told Dad the name of his father's horse or what color it was."

What are we to make of these three grandparents who returned from death for one last visit with those they had left behind? If one of our jobs in the hereafter is to watch over loved ones still on earth, who would take on this role more willingly than a doting grandmother or grand-father? And if spirits of the dead really do serve in this "guardian angel" capacity, maybe we should overcome our prejudice against them. After all, some ghosts are good guys.

# Fifteen

## This Property Is Condemned!

**N**ative Americans believe strongly that some places were never meant for human habitation and that to trespass in these areas, whether they are considered sacred or evil, is to invite disaster. A. J. Kalanick learned the wisdom of the Native Americans' belief when a routine job brought him face to face with some very eerie events in the summer of 1987.

The recording studio employing A.J. at the time had been contacted by a law firm. Some condominiums at the Big Sky ski resort north of West Yellowstone had been condemned after several years of occupation and A.J.'s job was to go inside the buildings to record the strange sounds that had been reported there.

"The builders had all kinds of problems from the very beginning," A.J. explained, "and the condos were substandard in a variety of ways. Because of faulty construction, there was so much pressure on the buildings that regular expansion and contraction from temperature changes caused them to make loud twisting sounds, so much so that anyone could tell they were unsafe. Most of these weird noises were loudest during sunrise and sunset."

In addition, there were electrical problems, the roofs leaked constantly, and the floors themselves were starting to give way. "And," A.J. added, "the studs in the walls had so much weight on them that if you flicked one with your finger it would sing like a guitar string."

Before the recordings could begin, A.J. had to make a trial inspection of the buildings to determine where to place the tape machines. Since he got there before the caretaker and the security officer who were to meet him, he spent some time walking around the parking lot and looking at the condemned structures.

There were two sets of buildings, each 150 to 200 yards long. The windows of the lower levels were boarded up and the one-time resort condos looked anything but inviting.

"It seemed odd standing in this empty parking lot and seeing these

buildings in the middle of a mountain," A.J. recalled. "I remember thinking at the time that they seemed unnatural and out of place."

He didn't have long to contemplate the strange buildings, however,
for suddenly he heard a man's voice speaking right behind him.

"What are you doing here?" it asked. Startled, A.J. whirled around
and found himself face to face with a Native American.

"I wondered where in the world he had come from," A.J. said, "since
I hadn't heard or seen him come up to me. He asked me again why I
was there, so I explained that I was waiting for the caretaker to let me
inside the building.

"'You're not supposed to be here,' the man said. So I explained that
I had an appointment with someone and a job to do. The mysterious
man just kept looking at me; then, finally, he spoke again. 'This is bad
medicine. Go away from here.'

"That's when I told him exactly what I was going to do," A.J. said,
"to record the sounds inside the condos so that those who had brought
the lawsuit could go ahead and have the buildings torn down. When I
explained this to my strange visitor, he finally told me what was bothering
him, that the condominiums had been constructed right next to Lone
Mountain, a pyramid-shaped formation that was sacred to his people.
After explaining this, he handed me a small leather pouch filled with
spruce needles and cedar bark.

"'Keep this with you,' he advised me. 'It will protect you.'

"I had dealt with other Native Americans in the past, and I've always
respected their ways," A.J. said. "So I told him I would keep the pouch
and I put it inside my pocket. And then the man just walked away."

Shortly afterward, the caretaker and the security guard showed up
to escort A.J. into the building. The guard was opening the door when
he suddenly admitted that he hated having to go inside.

"I asked him why," A.J. said, "and he told me that every time he
was in there the furniture seemed to have been moved around. That
seemed strange to me, because no one was supposed to be there."

The three men began walking through the buildings to find the best
places to set up the recording machinery. A.J. was immediately impressed
by the eerie atmosphere inside.

"All the doors had been left open, so you could walk in and out of
every unit in the building," he recalled. "It was very weird going through
all those places where people had been. Some of the tenants had moved
out and taken their belongings, of course, but other rooms looked as

if the people had suddenly just gotten up and abandoned everything. We even found magazines still on coffee tables and clothes still hanging in closets.

"We found the best places to set the tape recorders, locked up, and got out of there," A.J. continued. "My plan was to record from seven at night until seven in the morning and I was to go into the condos to flip the tapes or change them out every forty-five minutes.

"Everything was okay until about 7:00 P.M., when I got the creeps just thinking about walking alone through those buildings late at night. That's when I decided to call a friend to come up there and keep me company."

When A.J. and his friend finally entered the condos with only the light of a flashlight to guide their way, they both experienced a strange sensation. "It was as if we were being wrapped in a black blanket with something fluttering in front of our faces," he remembered. "And as we stood inside, we heard all the noises we had been told about. All buildings make shifting sounds, but these were like none we'd ever heard before. We heard creaks and pops and snaps so loud that sometimes they actually startled us and interrupted our conversation. There was also a horrible groaning, as if something were twisting and bending."

But peculiar noises weren't solely responsible for the gloomy mood of the neglected condos. Even though there had been no rain for weeks, water cascaded down the inside walls and the steps on the stairwell were soaked through and covered with mold.

During one of the brave climbs to the second floor to attend to the recorders there, the two friends made a discovery that has mystified them ever since. "As I mentioned before," A.J. pointed out, "the noises the buildings made were very, very loud. But when we played back the tape I had just recorded, all we could hear were the sounds that we had made. The only things audible were the sounds of the door shutting as I left the building, our voices as we walked through the rooms, and our footsteps as we approached the tape recorder. Even as we stood there listening to the recording, we heard the loud sounds of the building creaking and groaning, but those noises never showed up anywhere on the tape."

The mood became even eerier at three in the morning when the two men went in to change the tapes again. "That's when we were certain that the furniture had moved," A.J. said. "The first time I had gone to inspect the buildings, I noticed a couch about fifty feet from the door of the parking garage. Later I noticed that same couch sitting right next to the door. And, then, an hour and a half after that, the couch had turned around so that it was facing in the opposite direction.

"Other things had been tampered with upstairs too," he continued. "Earlier I had walked into some rooms close to where we were recording and I noticed that all the cupboard doors were closed and some chairs were sitting around on the floor. When I looked again at three o'clock, all the cupboard doors were open and the chairs were stacked on top of each other. Even as my eyes were seeing these things, I was trying to discount them and to tell myself that I had been mistaken.

"Things started getting really spooky at this point," A.J. recalled. "Once we were standing outside again, I told my friend, 'I really don't want to go back in there.' As I said that, I shone the flashlight across the face of one of the buildings and we both suddenly froze. There, looking out at us from a window on the upper floor, was a figure.

"It looked like a man wearing a white shirt and some kind of red-colored thing on his head, but what it was we couldn't make out. We stared at him for probably fifteen seconds. We thought at first that he might have been a transient, but whatever he was, we didn't dare risk going back into that building to find out.

"We contacted the sheriff's department immediately, and they came up with a couple of squad cars. They conducted a sweep of the whole building, but they found nobody inside. The strange thing was that there was no way for anyone to get in or out of the building other than through the door we had used. There was just no other access and we would have known if anyone had gotten in or out that way."

As soon as the last recordings were completed at seven that morning, A.J. and his friend left the spooky buildings. "I turned the tapes over to the law firm, but I doubt that they were much good to anybody. The strange noises that were so loud when we were inside the buildings just weren't on the tapes," A.J. said. "I've never figured that out, since the sounds were every bit as loud as our own voices."

The story doesn't end here, however. The same day A.J. returned from making the recordings, he ran into a friend who asked him where he had been. He told her and she said, "There's something following you around. I have a weird feeling about it." Then he told her about the Indian man who had given him the leather pouch of spruce needles and cedar bark and she said, "Go home and burn the cedar, and waft the smoke around to protect yourself against whatever it is that is following you."

A.J. did so, and since his strange experience at the condemned buildings at Big Sky he has thought many times about the mysterious Native American who brought him the leather pouch for protection. Perhaps the most significant thing about this encounter is that it fits into a pattern, for on two other occasions A.J. has also been approached by unknown Indians who have helped him in some way.

"Once when I was working and teaching at Montana State in Bozeman," he explained, "I was walking across campus when a voice behind me said, 'Excuse me, sir.' I turned around, and a Native American man told me, 'You need this. Give a portion of it to your lady.' He handed me a sprig of spruce and walked away before I had a chance to question him. The strange thing was that at that time I was indeed involved in a troubled love relationship.

"The other time occurred when I was in graduate school and was having trouble with my eyesight. I had begun having double vision, so that I had to squint, even with my glasses, to see clearly. The problem kept getting worse until finally I was seeing about seven shadowy images. I went to doctors, but they could find nothing wrong. Going to graduate school became almost impossible since I couldn't see well enough to read and had to absorb what I could just by listening in class.

"One day I was walking across campus when a Native American woman whom I'd never seen before suddenly walked up to me. Out of the blue she said, 'You're having problems with your eyesight.'

"I asked her how she knew that, but she just said, 'Never mind. You're going through a very difficult transition in your life and a lot of things are changing. As you complete this change, your sight will come back.'

"I asked her again how she knew this, and she said, 'Just don't worry. The change is very near. You're almost complete with this cycle.' Then she walked off and within two weeks my vision did come back."

How are we to explain such things as the eerie noises that failed to imprint themselves on tape and the encounters that A. J. Kalanick had with Native Americans who seemingly arrived from nowhere to help him in times of need? Some might suggest that the sounds emanating from the condemned condos had not so much to do with structural failure as with the fact that they were, as the mysterious Indian man claimed, built too close to the sacred mountain. Perhaps the sounds were not of this world at all; thus they could not break through the barriers necessary for them to register on earthly equipment. No one will ever know for sure now, since the condominiums were pulled down not long after A.J.'s experience with them. And what of the three Native Americans

111

who so mysteriously appeared to him? There are those who believe that we all have our spirit guides in the world beyond this one and that many of these special helpers were Native Americans in life. When we consider A. J. Kalanick's experience, we can't help but wonder whether this might not be true.

# Sixteen

# The Gracious Lady of the
# Grand Street Theater

If the folks at Helena's Grand Street Theater are right about their phantom's identity, the last thing she would want to do is to frighten anyone, especially the children who attend drama school there. For almost everyone familiar with the theater believes that the charming spirit in residence is Clara Bicknell Hodgin, a remarkable woman who had no children of her own, but who doted on the sons and daughters of other people.

Clara was the wife of the Reverend Edwin Stanton Hodgin, an early pastor of Helena's Unitarian church. One of Clara's greatest joys was putting on plays with her Sunday school classes and the church, with its stage and sloped floor, was ideal for dramatic presentations.

When Clara died suddenly and unexpectedly of a malignant abdominal tumor on January 14, 1905, she was only thirty-four years old. Her death left a void not only in Helena but in her native Humboldt, Iowa, as well. Before moving to Montana in 1903, Clara had taught in the public schools of Humboldt and former students there were so grief-stricken to hear of her death that they conducted their own service of remembrance. Many even wrote to Clara's parents, describing a teacher who sang and rocked them to sleep when they were ill or tired and who took pains to understand and encourage even the worst pupils. These tributes, along with others, were collected in a book titled *In Memoriam: Clara Bicknell Hodgin.*

Sorrowing friends in Helena raised five hundred dollars to commission another memorial, a stained-glass window designed by famous artist Louis Comfort Tiffany. Depicting a sunset in a mountain landscape suggestive of the Helena valley, the window was installed in the church in 1907. There it remained until 1933, when the Unitarians donated the building to the city.

The old church was converted into the Lewis and Clark Library and the Tiffany window was removed for safekeeping and stored in the

Clara Bicknell Hodgin, the charming woman whose spirit still graces
Helena's Grand Street Theater. (*Photograph courtesy Montana Historical
Society*)

basement of the Algerian Shrine Building, now the Civic Center. Incredibly, this work of art lay forgotten and virtually unprotected in a wooden crate for forty-three years.

It might have been lying there still if Helena stained-glass worker Paul Martin had not rediscovered it in 1976. While browsing through a record of all Tiffany windows created before 1910, he was surprised to learn that one had been installed in the old Unitarian church. With the help of townspeople who remembered seeing the window when they were young, Paul Martin located Clara's memorial and had it reinstalled in its original place on December 6, 1976, only a month after the newly established Grand Street Theater had held its first production in the building.

At least one report of psychic phenomena had surfaced when the former church was a library (Cora Poe heard phantom footsteps on a staircase directly over the boiler room), but when the theater took over the old building, the paranormal activity began in earnest and soon the Grand Street Theater was one of Montana's most famous haunted locales.

While the building was being renovated for use as a theater, Jerry Schneider heard ghostly footfalls on the front stairs. What made his experience even eerier was the fact that, at the time, the stairs had been removed and were not rebuilt until a few days later. And after the new stairs were in place, Grand Streeters heard the unexplained sounds two more times before the first show opened.

Through the years, ghostly footsteps have continued to resound in the lovely old building. Mary Vollmer Morrow, an actress and managerial assistant in the late seventies and early eighties, often heard someone coming through the front door, but when she went to check she discovered that she was alone. A few years later, two sisters, Joni Rodgers and Linda Darelius, heard the phantom striding across the stage one night when they knew they were the only people in the theater.

"We were building a dragon for the kids' production of *Five Chinese Brothers*," Joni told me, "and we were right underneath a trap door to the stage when we heard someone walking overhead. The sound wasn't muffled at all and there's no way we could have mistaken it for pipes rattling or anything else. The theater had been broken into twice before, so we went upstairs to make sure everything was okay. We didn't find anyone, so we went back to work downstairs.

"Shortly afterward, we heard someone run lightly across the stage," Joni continued. "Again we searched the entire theater, but no one was

The Grand Street Theater, formerly Helena's Unitarian church. (*Photograph courtesy George Lane*)

there. We were a little scared and started gathering our things to go when we heard more bumping and rustling noises overhead. We didn't want to go back upstairs to leave, so we just stepped out the door in the lower level."

In addition to her strolls around the theater in the wee hours, the ghost of the Grand Street also enjoys playing with the lights. The current director, Don McLaughlin, has a good story about something that occurred, appropriately enough, on Halloween 1985.

"I was working on the set for *Frankenstein* and part of it was a graveyard down stage left that stuck out into the house," he recalled. "To create a spooky effect, we used a flickering lamp and I plugged it into a cable with the dimmer off. There's no logical reason why the light should have come on when the dimmer was off, but it did. And odder still was the fact that the light stayed on even when I turned off the light board. When I left the theater that night, the flickering lamp was still on—when I came back the next morning, it had gone off. To this day, I can't explain what happened."

Costumer Aaron Haggins recalled that the lights and the radio in the costume shop have come on by themselves twice after being shut off, giving him the idea that the ghost didn't want to be left alone in the theater. This motive may also explain a weird series of events on a night in the mid-1980s when Ed Noonan was trying to lock up the building to leave.

"I was stage-managing a show, so I was the last person to go," he remembered. "I secured everything upstairs and left a stage light on before going downstairs. I hadn't been working long when I heard someone walking overhead. I went to see who it was, but I couldn't find anyone. I did notice, however, that the stage light had been turned off. I switched it back on, made sure that all the doors were locked, and returned downstairs to finish cleaning up.

"This same thing happened three times that night and, after I turned the stage light back on for the third time, I was convinced that the theater had a benevolent spirit who enjoyed playing tricks on people."

Nothing in Ed Noonan's assessment contradicts what is known about Clara Bicknell Hodgin. The tributes in her memorial book refer several times to her quick wit, ready laughter, and love of humor, and Ed is not the only Grand Streeter to have been on the receiving end of her pranks.

Joni Rodgers will never forget the elaborate practical joke played on her the night after a performance of *The Velveteen Rabbit*. "I was teaching drama school for kids in kindergarten through second grade," she said. "After the play, Janet McLaughlin and I were cleaning up and getting ready to leave. Before Janet left, she reminded me to lock the doors and to turn out the backstage light.

"I went backstage, turned off the light, and locked the front door," Joni continued. "Then I went to pick up the props to take them out to my car and I noticed that the backstage light was still on. I decided that I must have hit the wrong switch, so I put everything down and went to turn it off.

"When I returned to pick up the props to leave, I looked up, and guess what I saw? The backstage light was on again. I couldn't believe what was happening, so I went back to turn it off one more time. After I hit the switch, I walked onto the stage and saw the curtains moving as if the door were open and wind was blowing in. That's when I figured that Janet hadn't left after all and was playing a trick on me.

"I called out, 'Very funny, Janet! Knock it off—I need to get out of here.' I went back to the props and gathered everything up and called to her again. I didn't hear a response, but looked up to see the backstage light shining brightly.

"By this time, I was extremely annoyed," Joni confessed. "I yelled, 'Janet, cut it out! I have to go pick up my son.' I put everything down again and went to turn off the light for the third time. The curtains were still billowing and I heard a woman's laughter up in the balcony.

"I was sure that Janet was doing all of this and I was tired of being teased. I went to gather up the props and didn't even bother looking back to see whether or not the light stayed off.

"The next day when I saw her, I said, 'Very funny joke, Janet. The least you could have done was to help me carry my stuff out to the car and not make me go running back and forth ten times.' But she just looked at me strangely and said she had no idea what I was talking about. And, after all this time, Janet still swears that she had nothing to do with the weird events of that night."

Joni recalls another occasion, after a performance during the 1987 Christmas season, when the mischievous spook kept returning props to the stage just as fast as she and Marianne Adams could put them away. According to Marianne, this behavior was not unusual for the playful ghost.

"I'm sure that part of the problem was our own lack of organization," she admitted, "but sometimes things reappeared in the exact place where we'd already looked for them. And that was just a little too creepy."

One particularly uncanny occurrence in the mid-1980s still sends shivers down the spines of the folks at Grand Street. Late one night Mary Vollmer Morrow and scene designers Rick and Jackie Penrod were working on stage when they heard the sound of someone turning on the power saw and cutting wood in the shop below.

"We couldn't figure out who would have been down there at that time," Rick explained. "We went downstairs to look, but there was nobody in the shop and no sign that anyone had interfered with the tools. The saw wasn't even near any wood.

"We were a bit shaken by this, so we went home. Later, we asked all the people who could possibly have been there if they'd been using the saw that night. They all denied it and we still don't have an explanation for what happened. I suppose we could have heard a sound from somewhere else but, at the time, we were sure that the noise was coming from the shop."

Because some of the strange manifestations at Grand Street have involved electrical equipment, a few people believe that the phantom is that of a man, perhaps a former janitor. If these people knew more about Clara, however, they would certainly agree that a fascination with gadgets would not have been unusual for such a progressive woman. Friends and acquaintances who wrote their tributes repeatedly mentioned Clara's brilliant intellect, unstinting capacity for hard work, and her "remarkable executive ability." Such a spirit would hardly be daunted by power tools or electric lights—in fact, she probably appreciates the improvements made on these devices since her day.

Another gizmo Clara apparently found engrossing was a fire extinguisher hanging on a wall on stage right. "I was playing Titania in *A Midsummer Night's Dream* five or six years ago," recalled Kathryn O'Connell. "I was standing next to the fire extinguisher, doing some warmup stretches before going back on stage. I reached my head out to stretch my back and, as I did so, that fire extinguisher began to swing like nobody's business, back and forth like a pendulum. I was really frightened, because I realized that even if there had been wind in the building, it wouldn't explain the weird motions this thing was making.

"I stared at the fire extinguisher and wondered if I were dreaming or imagining things. Finally, I spoke out loud, saying 'Stop!' Surprisingly, the movement ceased. Then I hightailed it out of there."

Kathryn remembers another strange incident that occurred when she was stage-managing a production back in the late 1970s. "I was getting ready to leave the theater and I had just locked all the doors, including the one to the shop," she said. "Suddenly, it sounded as if all the boards stored in there were falling down and then I heard someone running across the floor. Because I had just locked all the doors, the only way anyone could have gotten out of the building was right past where I was standing. But I saw nobody go by."

Mary Vollmer Morrow has heard doors opening and shutting and keys jangling on the stairwell when she knew she was alone in the theater and Jean Hardie remembers hearing "horrible creaking sounds" when she and her husband and daughter spent three nights there. "We had some expensive sound equipment at Grand Street, so for a while people took turns sleeping in the building to protect it," she explained. "As soon as the lights went off, the creaking and groaning sounds began and since we knew we were alone in the place we attributed them to the ghost."

Jean's husband Pete was the technical director and, in keeping with a widespread theater tradition, he always turned on one special bulb known as the "ghost light" during productions. This tradition is commonly performed to keep phantoms at bay. "But when we were trying to sleep, the ghost light wasn't even plugged in," Jean said.

In 1990, costumer Karen Loos heard something even more startling than creaks and groans. "We were having a dress rehearsal for the play *Voice of the Prairie* and I was in no mood to be distracted by anything," she recalled. "I was downstairs in the costume storage room scrambling to find replacements for something. That's when I distinctly heard a woman's voice saying my first name, from no farther away than six inches behind my head. I spun around, but the room was empty. I went back to looking for the costume and when I started to walk up the stairway, I heard the voice call my name again.

"I searched around for whoever might have been looking for me, but I found no one," Karen continued. "I wasn't frightened, but I just turned around and said, 'Hi, ghost; I've got no time right now.'"

It was during this same play that a Carroll College student reported seeing an apparition in the theater. "After the performance was over, we left the building, and my friend told me he'd seen a ghost," said Debra Dacar, also a student at Carroll. "At first I didn't believe him, but he insisted that during the middle of the play he'd seen the white, glowing face of a woman floating up in the rafters, on the right-hand side facing the stage."

Apparitions are rare at the theater, although Kathryn O'Connell once saw a bluish white light coming down some stairs. Far more commonly reported is the feeling of an unseen presence and, although the very idea of a ghost tends to be unnerving, most of the cast and crew at Grand Street have come to regard Clara as a protective, albeit mischievous, guardian spirit.

Before knowing anything about the supposed identity of the ghost, Grace Gardiner felt sure that it was a female with a strong interest in drama. Grace has sensed Clara's presence on several occasions, mainly when she was alone in the building.

"The first night I felt her near me was six or seven years ago when I was stage-managing a show," she recalled. "Although I was by myself, I could have sworn that another person was there with me. I'm a pretty rational person, generally not one to believe in the supernatural, but I definitely had the feeling that if I turned around I'd see someone."

Grace felt frightened on this first encounter, but since then, she's gotten used to Clara. "I always have the feeling that she's slightly above me, hovering over my right shoulder," Grace explained. "I also believe that she watches our rehearsals from up in the balcony, especially when we have a small cast. I think her real interest is in putting a show together— maybe that's why she tries her hand at playing with the light board or moving things around on prop tables."

Clara has also been known to talk to actors before they go on stage and she has tapped their shoulders in the middle of a performance. And, according to Aaron Haggins, one former costumer felt someone step on the hem of her long dress as she walked across the stage. From time to time, this same woman often felt a mysterious cold spot on the back stairway near where the pastor's office used to be.

Like Grace Gardiner, Sidney Poole has stage-managed several shows and she agrees that the ghost is always fun-loving, never threatening. "I'm very comfortable with the idea of guardian spirits," said Sidney, "and the fact that one seems to reside in our theater should be comforting, not scary."

Sidney has felt the presence of Clara on several occasions, but she has experienced only one thing out of the ordinary. "I knocked a 'wet paint' sign to the floor when I entered what we call the dungeon, our prop room under the front steps," she explained. "When I left the furnace room, I found the sign on the bench next to the door and I have no idea how it got there."

Sidney's thirteen-year-old son Dan also felt the watchful presence of the phantom when he attended the Grand Street Theater School of Dance, and Marianne Adams even credits Clara with helping her to give up smoking.

"In the summer of 1987 I spent a lot of time by myself in the theater," she said, "and whenever I tried to light a cigarette, my match didn't just sputter out—somebody seemed to blow it out. This happened more than ten times and it finally dawned on me that the ghost was trying to make me quit smoking.

"This and other experiences have led me to believe that the spirit has maternal feelings for the people at Grand Street, especially for the kids who come here," Marianne continued. "During the 1990 Christmas season, a two-year-old girl was tagging along with me, when she realized that she had lost her sweater. I remembered that she'd had it on earlier and we searched everywhere and still couldn't find it. Finally, I looked inside the girl's toy pack and there was the sweater, folded neatly. I asked around, but no one in the theater had placed it there. And, obviously, it was folded far too perfectly for a two-year-old to have done it herself."

It seems ludicrous for anyone to be afraid of such a gentle, motherly spirit, but the common prejudice against ghosts is that, if they exist at all, they must be frightening, especially to small children. Such an attitude must bother the kind-hearted Clara, who labored all her short life to bring knowledge, beauty, and humor into the lives of young people. And even though she has passed from this world to the next, who can blame her if from time to time she returns to enjoy her Tiffany window and to visit the scene of so many earthly delights.

# Seventeen

# Spooks Galore in Mining City Mansions

The mining city of Butte, Montana, has more than its share of spook-ridden houses, but that's only to be expected in a city so vital to the development of the West. In many ways, the history of Butte is the history of Montana itself, so it's no wonder that the spirits of some who developed the town named for the "Richest Hill on Earth" should still choose to reside there.

Ghosts in general tend to have poor reputations, but some of these citizens of early-day Butte are far from unwelcome in the homes they continue to inhabit. Ann Cote-Smith, who lives in Senator W. A. Clark's "Copper King" Mansion, couldn't be happier that the shade of the original owner still seems to be around.*

An article that appeared in the Halloween 1979 edition of Butte's *Montana Standard* doesn't do justice to the benevolent spirit who watches over the living residents of the Copper King Mansion. Titled "Shades of Amityville stalk Mining City homes," the story by Andrea McCormick likens the phenomena at the Clark Mansion and two other unidentified Butte homes to the horrific goings-on at the New York haunted house made famous by the book and movie, both titled *The Amityville Horror*. At least in the case of the Copper King Mansion, the analogy doesn't work. For as Ann Cote-Smith herself explained, "I feel safer here than I would inside the Rock of Gibraltar."

The thirty-two-room red brick Victorian showplace at 219 West Granite took four years to build and was finally finished in 1888. Ann has lived in the house, now a restaurant and a bed and breakfast establishment, since her mother purchased it from the bishop of Helena in 1952.

"The house has a wonderful presence in it," Ann insisted. "The Copper King Mansion was a convent for seventeen years and during that time

---

*Mrs. Ann Cote-Smith died soon after this manuscript was completed. Her niece, Maria Wagner, has taken over as curator of the Copper King Mansion.

W. A. Clark's "Copper King" mansion in Butte, where the protective ghost of the original owner imparts a feeling of happiness to current residents and guests. (©*Rainbow Photo, Butte, Montana*)

a mass was said here every day. The nuns had a chapel in the house and we have one too, although not in the same room. We accumulated so many religious articles from various churches here in Butte that we needed a larger room, so we moved the chapel into an upstairs area right off the ballroom.

"I think that the existence of the chapel might be what gives us this wonderful feeling of protection," Ann explained, "both for the people in the house and the house itself. I'm a person who is leery of staying in a motel by myself in a strange town, but I'm never afraid here, even when I'm the only person at home. Only good things have happened here; the Copper King Mansion has brought a lot of joy to many people, not only to the ones who have lived here, but to visitors who come for tours or for dinner or to spend the night.

"I've talked to guests who have told me, 'This is the happiest place; there's so much joy in the house itself.' And even though there have always been rumors that the Copper King Mansion is haunted, we know that we have a very friendly ghost."

As the *Montana Standard* article indicates, the game room in the mansion stays dark and cold no matter how bright the lights are or how high the heat is turned up. "This room is always chilly and that seems strange," Ann admitted to me. "We keep the temperature in the house at seventy-eight degrees, but it never seems to get above sixty-eight in the game room. Also, there's a bathroom off this room and tour guides tell me that they can never keep the door to it open. They keep propping it to stay ajar, but it's always closed when they return."

On other occasions doors that have been left open will be found locked and lights turned off the night before have been discovered on again the next morning. Ann has also heard footsteps on the stairs when no one was there.

The master bedroom where she sleeps is directly over the dining room and tour groups walking on the bedroom floor often cause a tinkling of the crystal chandelier below. "But sometimes this occurs when nobody is upstairs," Ann explained, "and we always blame the ghost. I had a wonderful friend who lived with me for several years before she died and whenever the chandelier would tinkle or any other unusual thing would happen, she'd look over her shoulder and say, 'Come on, now, W. A. We don't need any of this foolishness today—we've got too much work to do.'"

Occasionally Ann's tiny poodle, only a foot and a half high, runs to a room and barks for no obvious reason, but Ann's daughter Clancy Stockham attributes the dog's behavior to its keen sense of hearing, rather than to any psychic phenomena.

Clancy grew up in the mansion, moved away when she reached adulthood, and returned to live with her mother just a couple of years ago. Clancy likens the kindly presence in the house to a guardian angel, but she added, "I certainly can understand why tour guides and people who don't live here can become spooked, because we have a hot water radiator system that hisses and clangs and bangs. It sounds like a regular symphony when the furnace goes on."

Clancy also thinks that people expect big houses to be haunted. "We have so many rooms here that people wonder about what may be going on in different parts of the house that they can't see," she said. "There's something about large homes that makes people nervous."

A man named Ken, who is still employed by Ann Cote-Smith and who lived in the mansion for several years, is apparently the only person who has actually seen the ghost and even on those occasions he has witnessed only quick glimpses of something white. "There's definitely a spirit in this house," he said. "I can feel it and sometimes I see flashes of shadow or a light-colored thing that floats and moves around. I've seen it in the basement, as well as on the first floor, but I've never seen it on the second or third floor. I did see it once on the second stair landing and, as I was watching, it moved up a little bit so that I couldn't see it anymore.

"I believe that it's the spirit of W. A. Clark and he's just checking his house to make sure it's safe and sound," Ken added. "And whenever I see the apparition, I take it as an omen that I'm going to have a good day, and I usually do."

Ann Cote-Smith invites all ghost aficionados to check out the happy phantom for themselves. "They can stop by for dinner," she said, "and if they tell us they're interested in spooks, we'll see if we can rustle one up for them."

Other spirits who are equally welcome in their old abode are those at the Hennessy Mansion, currently the home of Tom and Beverly George. The gorgeous house on the corner of Park and Excelsior was built in the early years of the twentieth century by D. J. Hennessy, founder of the Hennessy department store chain. Several families succeeded the original owners in the mansion and the structure also served at different times as a dormitory for nursing students at the Catholic hospital and as a fraternity house for students at the Montana College of Mineral Science and Technology. The Georges moved into the home about sixteen years ago and since then have put a lot of effort into restoring the mansion to its former grandeur.

Their friend Patrick Judd believes that the most commonly encountered ghost in the house is none other than D. J. Hennessy himself and that his presence shows his curiosity about the work the Georges have done. "The house was severely damaged when my friends bought it," Patrick explained. "The fraternity boys had no respect for the place at all and they trashed it badly. They got drunk and knocked the spindles out of the staircases and burned them in the fireplace. I don't know if they encountered the ghost or not, but very soon after the Georges bought the place, we realized that a mysterious male presence was still here.

"I think Mr. Hennessy was just waiting for someone to come along who would love the house and take proper care of it," Patrick said. "He got to enjoy the mansion for such a short time before he died suddenly and my guess is that he wasn't ready to leave."

Pat has never seen Hennessy's spirit, but he has sensed its presence on several occasions. "The house has four stories, including a full basement (with hardwood floors) that doubled as a ballroom and gymnasium," he explained. "It's not a dark, dingy basement at all; it has windows on two

A window of Butte's Copper King Mansion. This photograph, taken in 1990, shows what appears to be the upside-down image of a sailing ship in the window. Photographer Tony DiFronzo says no such figure was visible in the window when he took this photo, nor does he know how anyone could re-create it. (*Photograph courtesy Tony DiFronzo*)

......

sides, so it's a relatively bright place. The sense of Mr. Hennessy's presence is strongest when you come down the staircase leading to the gym and around the corner to an enclosed landing. Here, windows look into the workout room and at this spot the feeling is most intense. It's not a frightening sensation and you don't feel it all the time, but it's fairly common.

"About a year after the Georges moved in, I was house sitting for them while they were on a trip," Pat remembered. "They shipped a big van full of antique French and Spanish furniture to the mansion and I told the movers to place the pieces in various spots around the rooms where they would be safe for the time being.

"Tom and Beverly called to tell me they would be home the next day, so I started dusting and doing some work in the kitchen. All of a sudden, I got goose bumps on the back of my neck and I sensed that someone was standing at the kitchen door at the top of the staircase.

"At first I tried to ignore the feeling, but it kept getting stronger and stronger. This went on for about twenty minutes, until finally I got angry. I said, 'Mr. Hennessy, leave me alone—I've got work to do.' Then I slammed the kitchen door and that was the end of it.

"I didn't say anything to the Georges when they got home, but I returned for a visit the day after they came back," Pat continued. "We were sitting there talking when Mrs. George asked me, 'By the way, when did Mr. Hennessy start coming up from the basement?' She told me that she had gotten up in the middle of the night to get something to drink and the presence had been in the downstairs hallway.

"I told her that he must have been curious about what was going on in the house, because until all this museum quality furniture arrived, he had just stayed down in the gymnasium," Pat said. "He seemed to spend quite a lot of time exploring the house after that. Every time a new restoration project was finished, he'd come to check it out. I believe he's content that someone is finally trying to put the house back together, because he hasn't come up from the basement for quite a while now. I haven't felt the presence for over a year."

Pat added that Mrs. George has encountered both Mr. Hennessy and the other spirit in the house, but she didn't want to talk about her experiences. No one is sure who the other ghost is, but it is definitely that of a woman and she has a long history in the mansion.

"After the Hennessy family left, at some time another family bought the house," Pat said. "Their daughters would be very elderly now, if they're still living, but the story is that they sometimes woke up to see the lady ghost sitting on the end of their bed, just watching them. She always appeared in a bedroom on the second floor and that's where Mrs. George encountered her too. The phantom apparently has never tried to communicate and she doesn't seem unhappy—she just appears. She might be Mrs. Hennessy, but no one knows for sure, and not even the little girls were frightened of her."

In contrast to the benign spirits of the Copper King and Hennessy mansions, others haunt selected homes around Butte. Patrick Judd remembers having some particularly unpleasant feelings at the home of some friends whom he didn't want to name.

"I'm not sure, in fact, that what I encountered was actually a ghost," he explained. "Instead, it might have been a kind of trap of negative emotions. But these friends of mine had bought an old home on the West Side, below Park Street. It was just a few blocks from the Hennessy Mansion and I would guess the house was built sometime between 1905 and 1915. The main floor is a stone structure and the second and third stories are clapboard.

"My friends moved in and immediately began redecorating the interior," Patrick continued. "When they finished making it beautiful, they had a dinner party and invited several friends over to see the house. Right away, I could tell that the woman was not happy there. While she was giving us a tour, she pulled me aside and said, 'Come here. I want you to see something.'

"She took me up to the third floor nursery area and right at the top of the third floor staircase was a small landing about four feet square," Pat explained. "On the right were two steps up into what had been the nanny's bedroom and on the left were two steps up to the suite of rooms that had belonged to the children.

"My hostess didn't say anything, but as soon as I got to the third floor landing I felt something almost like a physical blow, as if someone were trying to push me down the stairs. That seemed very strange, but I decided that I had been mistaken and that I had just lost my balance. My friend went on to show me the upstairs and then she took me back to the bottom of the third floor staircase where there was a door into what had been a kind of office. Under the staircase is a closet and my friend told me to go into the room and then to look in the closet. I noticed that she didn't accompany me.

"No one had even mentioned anything about ghosts, but as soon as I opened the closet door I felt a deep but inexplicable despair. I walked out of there and said only that it was a nice room.

"My friend took one look at me and asked, 'You felt it, too, didn't you?'

"I said, 'What do you mean—the closet? And at the top of the stairs?'

"She said, 'Yes. I can't stand it. We're going to sell this place.'

"My friend did some research and discovered that all the members of the family who had built the house were apparently still living. But when the children were little, their father had been extremely abusive," Pat explained. "He threw them down the staircase and locked them in the closet for days on end. I believe that he is dead now, but at one time he was a respected Butte doctor. It seems that he and his children must have left an incredible amount of energy on the staircase and in the closet. My friend said that on four or five occasions she too had felt something grab her and try to shove her down the stairs. Oddly enough, her children never experienced this and neither did her husband. Fortunately, they were able to sell the house and move out, even though they were initially worried about finding a buyer."

No less an ordeal was experienced by the unidentified families who lived in the two homes featured alongside the Copper King Mansion in the Halloween 1979 *Montana Standard* article. The first house is described only as "an attractive, two-story brick home on the upper West Side." An elderly woman had died in the house only a short time before a Butte family moved in and stayed only a year or so before eerie occurrences forced them out.

At first, nothing seemed unusual except that the family's dog refused to go upstairs even if someone went with him. Then the people began hearing someone walking around upstairs when no one was there. The mother rearranged items that had belonged to the previous owner and found them later back in their original places.

The family took their troubles to the landlord, expecting to discover that he knew some secret entrance into the house and had somehow been the cause of the mysterious phenomena. But he denied that there was any hidden entryway and he claimed to know nothing about the disturbances.

In the meantime, the walking sounds continued at odd times of the day and night and no one was ever found who could be making them. The footsteps seemed to be coming from the master bedroom, which had been converted into a playroom. The children thought the room was scary and never wanted to play there and later it became the scene of an even stranger incident.

There was a collection of old irons in the kitchen, the kind that had to be heated on the stove. The family left the house one day and when they returned they found one of the irons in the playroom. It had been thrown through a plastic doll buggy belonging to one of the daughters. The girl who owned the buggy blamed one of her sisters, who in turn swore that she was innocent.

The phenomena in the house became even more frightening one evening when the mother and three daughters were watching television. The dog began whining and pacing and at the same time the walking sounds started upstairs. The pace of the footsteps became faster and faster and louder and louder, without letting up. Finally, the children were so terrified that their mother took them to the home of a relative. The mother and the children's grandfather returned to the house to search from the attic to the basement for the source of the noise, but they found nothing. All the while, the frantic walking continued.

The family was also plagued by windows and doors that opened and closed for no reason and they finally decided to move out. But, even years after leaving the house, the mother said that she still got frightened when she thought about what had happened there.

The other house mentioned in the newspaper article was described as "an unassuming, two-story brick house on the lower West Side." It had been built around the beginning of the twentieth century by a Butte attorney and his wife and they raised three daughters there. The youngest child married, had a son, and divorced, before moving back in with her parents. She later became ill and died, as did her parents at a later date.

The house was vacant for several years until 1955, when another family bought it. The old dwelling was in need of much repair and it took this second family a year just to make it comfortable. A series of unexplained phenomena made life difficult for them, but they couldn't afford to move. They weren't able to leave for almost twenty years, until they finally sold the property in 1974.

The house, the family, and the phenomena described in this article all sound the same as those in a chapter of D. F. Curran's 1986 booklet, *True Hauntings in Montana*. I was unable to contact Curran, but the details of the two stories are so similar that they must pertain to the same house and family. For that reason, I have combined the details of the two accounts.

The unusual phenomena began occurring even before the family (given the pseudonym of "Reardon" by Curran) were able to settle into their new home. Early one Saturday morning the parents arrived with tools, paint samples, and some furniture. They had no sooner made a pot of coffee in the kitchen than they heard walking noises overhead. The footsteps continued and then descended the stairs. Believing that an intruder was in the house, Mr. and Mrs. Reardon cautiously walked to the bottom of the stairs, where they were shocked to find no one.

The phantom footsteps were to trouble the Reardons for the rest of their stay in the house. Two daughters shared an upstairs bedroom across from an attic area and one night while they were in the living room they heard the walking begin in the attic. The attic door opened and closed and the footsteps continued down the stairs and into the kitchen. The pantry door and then the swinging door into the dining room were opened, and the dog began growling, seeming to watch as someone invisible crossed the room. The walking continued into the hall off the dining room and when the door to the master bedroom flew open the girls ran outside in terror.

On another occasion after the Reardons were in bed, the footsteps and door-closing routine started in the kitchen and the sounds of a man's heavy footsteps proceeded quickly up the stairs, accompanied by the noise of jingling keys or coins. Both the mother and one of the daughters heard the sounds, but when they switched on the lights they could see no one.

Another spooky incident occurred when the Reardons held a party in the dining room. Suddenly, something turned off the light switch, making the room completely dark. A mysterious scent of flowers was in the air and the doors began opening and closing for no apparent reason. At the same time, the Reardons and their guests all heard the sounds of footsteps in the attic and the upstairs bedroom.

Also unaccounted for were frequent knocking sounds in the bathroom walls and on doors and windows, witnessed by many family members. One day the front door opened and closed on its own and both this door and the storm door, which had been locked, were found unlocked afterward. There was also the occasional smell of pipe tobacco, even though none of the family smoked a pipe, and the dog continued to growl and watch figures that were invisible to the people. Sometimes the thermostat would be turned way up high and everyone denied tampering with it.

Strangest of all was a Christmas card with five dollars that disappeared from the tree. In spite of a family search, the card was not found until many months later, when it reappeared, the money intact, in an unused writing desk in the attic.

Once in the middle of the night, Mr. Reardon awoke to see the faint figure of a man standing at the foot of his bed, wearing a strange dark costume and reeking of pipe tobacco. The phantom reached out to touch the man's feet through the blankets. At the same time, a cold draft filled the room. Experiences similar to this were to happen many times to Mr. Reardon, who was also occasionally awakened by a tapping on his leg.

One of the daughters was awakened in the same bedroom by a slap across her cheeks and, at another time, her sister was poked in the ribs, then punched in the face.

This sister and her first husband stayed in the room in later years and the husband claimed that he had awakened to see a man wearing what looked like a pilgrim's cap, a cape, and a sword. His wife didn't believe him until a next-door neighbor who heard the description said that it sounded very much like the costume worn by the original owner, who belonged to the Knights Templar.

If the unpleasant spirit in the Reardons' house was truly that of the former owner, they never learned why he wanted to torment them. It is perhaps significant, however, that in many ways the two families were strikingly similar. Each had three daughters and, in each case, the youngest had married, given birth to a son, divorced, and returned home. The deed to the house explained how much the first family had loved their grandson and it stated explicitly that their former son-in-law was to be denied any claim to the boy. The Reardons felt equally strongly about their grandchild and they too wanted to keep their ex-son-in-law away from him.

Remarkable as the similarities between the two families are, they don't appear to be reason enough for the eerie phenomena in the house. The Reardons at one time held a seance in their kitchen, bringing a picture of the former owner down from the attic. A chill descended on the family and a man in dark clothing began moving toward them. Terrified, the Reardons snapped on the lights, causing both the cold feeling and the ghost to disappear instantly.

D. F. Curran's account mentions another incident that may or may not have been caused by paranormal phenomena. Mr. and Mrs. Reardon were getting ready to go to a meeting one night when Mrs. Reardon became ill and lay down on the couch. She was unable to move or to speak and her body became cold and numb. Her frantic husband was unable to get a response from her, but she heard everything he said. The woman's strange paralysis ended after an hour and she apparently suffered no further effects. The ghost may conceivably have been to blame in this episode, but it seems more likely that Mrs. Reardon may have suffered some kind of stroke.

Desperate to get away from all the weird manifestations, the family finally sold their home after ten unsuccessful attempts. They found a buyer only after locking hands and praying that someone would relieve them of the property. A week later the house and all its problems belonged to new owners. Curran's account claims that since the Reardons sold it, no one has been able to stay in the house for any length of time.

In a city such as Butte where so much history has been played out, there are probably ten times more haunted houses than are presented in this chapter. In fact, one frustration of trying to put together a collection of ghost stories is that often the best ones go unreported or, even if someone does make them public, the facts are elusive and practically impossible to confirm.

One story told to me by Tim Gordon, whose other experiences are described elsewhere in this book, is too good not to include, even though there was no way to verify it.

Tim and one of his brothers were spending the day in Butte looking for antiques and one of the places they stopped was an older two-story house; the woman living there had responded to Tim's ad in the newspaper. The lower floor of her home had been made into an apartment and she augmented her income from this rental. At that particular time, no one was living in the apartment and, after buying antiques upstairs, Tim asked whether she had anything to sell downstairs.

"She took us down there and we saw a beautiful Victorian hobby horse," Tim explained. "It was a very desirable piece, easily worth several hundred dollars. We asked her if she would sell it, and she refused. We started making offers and got up to quite a high figure when she suddenly admitted that it wasn't for sale.

"By this time, we'd developed quite a rapport with her, so she told us the story connected with the hobby horse. She didn't tell us how she had come to own it, but she said that whenever anyone tried to take it out of the apartment, the sound of a child crying could be heard coming from the basement.

"Her story struck me as being absolutely true," Tim concluded, "especially since it was clear that she wouldn't sell the hobby horse for any price."

Who was the mysterious ghostly child who cried whenever the toy was removed from the house? We'll probably never know the details surrounding this charming story, but it too lingers as a legacy from the Mining City's prosperous and turbulent past.

# Appendix: Additional Readings

Debra D. Munn, *Ghosts on the Range: Eerie True Tales of Wyoming* (Boulder, Colo.: Pruett Publishing Company, 1989). My previous collection contains "The Extraordinary Tale of Chief Black Foot," a story set in both Wyoming and Montana. The Rev. Victoria Mauricio was visited by the spirit of Chief Black Foot, a Crow Indian, who wanted her to find his remains near Meeteetse, Wyoming, and arrange for their reburial on his tribal land in Montana.

Victoria Mauricio, *The Return of Chief Black Foot* (Virginia Beach/ Norfolk, Va.: Donning, 1981). The author tells her own story of the account described above.

Earl Murray, *Ghosts of the Old West* (Chicago: Contemporary Books, 1988). This fine collection contains three stories set in Montana: "Visions of Reno Crossing," about the Little Bighorn Battlefield; "The Hot Springs Phantom," about Chico Hot Springs; and "The Mysteries of Old Garnet." In addition, in "The Mystery of the Little People," Murray discusses the legendary small beings believed to be protectors of the Crow tribe. In "La Llorona, the Weeping Woman," he describes a phantom well known to large numbers of Hispanic people, mostly in the Southwest. However, Murray points out that "the migration of Hispanics as far north as Billings, Montana, has brought La Llorona to the banks of the Yellowstone River, where some have seen her wandering through the cottonwoods there" (108).

Edward Garcia Kraul and Judith Beatty, eds., *The Weeping Woman: Encounters with La Llorona* (Santa Fe, N.Mex.: The Word Process, 1988). This collection contains nearly fifty stories told by people who have come in contact with the wailing woman phantom of the Southwest.

Ray John de Aragon, *The Legend of La Llorona* (Las Vegas, N.Mex.: The Pan American Publishing Company, 1980). The author presents his scholarly research on La Llorona and then weaves his own story about her from tales told by descendants of the early Spanish colonists.

Deborah L. Downer, ed., *Classic American Ghost Stories* (Little Rock, Ark.: August House Publishers, Inc., 1990). The editor has brought together supposedly true stories from newspapers, journals, and magazines, and one of them, "Heavy Collar and the Ghost Woman," is set in Montana. This tale concerns a female spirit in skeletal form who followed a man wherever he went. Originally, the story by George Bird Grinnell appeared in *Blackfoot Lodge Tales: The Story of a Prairie People* (Lincoln, Nebr.: University of Nebraska Press, 1962).

D. F. Curran, *True Hauntings in Montana* (Missoula, Mont.: D. F. Curran Productions, 1986). This comic book–style publication contains eleven chapters and one short story about Montana's spooks and related themes. "Garnet," "Phillipsburg [*sic*]," "Butte," and "Drawer" contain stories that also appear in the book you are holding in your hands. Other chapters specifically on the subject of ghosts are described as follows:

"Billings" is about a two-story house on First Avenue North, supposedly haunted by a young girl named Beverly who died in a fall on the stairs early in the century. No real names or addresses are given. Since I was unable to contact Curran, I could not investigate this story.

"Judith Gap" similarly concerns an anonymous two-story house that is the haunt of a mischievous ghost in that town. I wrote to Ken and Patti Kowalczyk, owners of the Judith Gap Mercantile, but neither they nor anyone with whom they spoke about the matter could tell which house is featured in the chapter.

"Old Hag (#1)" takes place in the Target Range area of Missoula and involves an anonymous student at the University of Montana. He experienced presences in his bedroom at night that left him exhausted and listless.

"Violet" is set in a small, unnamed mountain town. An elderly woman moved in with friends and told stories of her Wild West days when she and her friend Violet O'Hara were young. When Violet died, the elderly woman asked her male friend to help her dispose of Violet's possessions. When the man picked up a pile of pressed flowers, he saw the ghostly face of Violet from an upstairs window.

Marty Kelly, "The Door-Stop Skull," *True West*, 1 (Fall 1953). Reprinted 6 (February 1959). In the process of burying their loot, the notorious Shelby clan dug up an Indian grave in the Highwood Mountains. They took home a skull to use as a doorstop and ignored warnings from their father about the dire consequences of such an act. His prophecy proved accurate, as practically the whole family died tragically.

John D. Ellingsen, *The Legend of the House in White Sulphur: A Bit of*

*Montana Folklore* (Bozeman, Mont.: Montana State University, 1966). (Now available on microfilm.) This fictional tale was inspired by the author's trip to an actual house known as "The Castle" in White Sulphur Springs.

Roberta Donovan and Keith Wolverton, *Mystery Stalks the Prairie* (Raynesford: THAR, 1976). Primarily about UFOs, this book also mentions phantom helicopters and a phantom automobile. Both, however, are probably not true ghost stories, but are instead somehow connected to the UFO and cattle mutilation phenomena. The account of the ghostly car is as follows:

> [A Bozeman man] said he was driving south of Augusta just before dark on February 6, 1976, when he noticed a car about a half mile behind him. He said the area was flat with no turnoffs from the highway. He had been looking into his rear view mirror frequently, and this car seemed to *"appear out of nowhere."*
>
> He said the car followed him for six or seven miles, so when he came to a turnoff, he pulled off to wait for it to go by. There was a dip in the highway just before the turnoff and he waited for the car to come out of the dip, but it didn't.
>
> He finally continued on down the road and the car appeared again. When he reached Bowman's Corner, he pulled off again and waited for it to go by, but again it never appeared.
>
> By strange coincidence, the same thing happened to his employer on an earlier night, in almost the exact same spot. (86)

# Index

Ace Refrigeration, Missoula, Mont., 45
Adams, Marianne, 118, 121
Albany, N.Y., 27
Albertson, Joe (pseudonym), 59, 60
Albertson, Louise (pseudonym), 59, 60–61
Algerian Shrine Building, Helena, Mont., 115
*American Heritage,* 64
*Amityville Horror, The,* 123
"An Historian Looks at Custer," 52
Apartment A, Little Bighorn Battlefield National Monument, 62–63
Apartment C, Little Bighorn Battlefield National Monument, 64–65
Apartment D, Little Bighorn Battlefield National Monument, 61
*Applied Psi,* 70
Aragon, Ray John de, 137
Arizona Memorial Museum Association in Hawaii, 60
Augusta, Mont., 139
Ayers, Bill, 100

Bank Exchange Saloon, Bannack, Mont., 18
*Bannack: Cradle of Montana,* 14
Bannack, Mont., 1, 14–18
Barrows, John, 15
Bearmouth, Mont., 2
Beatty, Judith, 137
Benteen, Captain Frederick, 50, 51
Bernardis, Tim, 61–62, 64, 65
Bessette, Amede, 14, 15
"Beverly" (pseudonym), 138
Big Draw, 28
Big Horn County, 56
Big Sky ski resort, 107–12
Billings, Mont., 2, 19, 137, 138

Bisch, Theodore, 40
Black Foot, Chief, 137
*Blackfoot Lodge Tales: The Story of a Prairie People,* 138
Black Horse Lake, 29–31
Bob Marshall Wilderness Area, 5
Bone Basin, 40–41
Boone, Daniel, 34–35, 38
Botzer, Sergeant Edward, 64
Bouchard, Joyce, 100
Boulder, Colo., 137
Boulder Country Corral of Westerners, 52
Boulder Hot Springs, Boulder, Mont., 2
Bowen, Fred, 78
Bowen, Leonard, 78
Bowen, William, 78
Bowers, James F., 52–53
Bowker, R. G., 68–69
Bowman's Corner, 139
Bozeman, Mont., 19, 111, 139
Brantly Hall, University of Montana, Missoula, 34–35
Breckenridge Street, Helena, Mont., 26
Brockton, Mont., 4
*Butte Miner,* 86–97
Butte, Mont., 4, 5, 6, 80, 86–101, 103, 123–35, 138
Butte–Silver Bow County Courthouse, 1, 86–101

Carmer, Carl, 26
Carrhart House, Bannack, Mont., 18
Carroll College, Helena, Mont., 9–13, 120
Carroll, John M., 66
Carter, Phil, 27
"Castle, The," White Sulphur Springs, Mont., 139

Catlow Movers, 42

Cemetery Ridge, Little Bighorn Battlefield National Monument, 69

Chapin, Peter, 86

Chicago, Ill., 75, 137

Chico Hot Springs, Pray, Mont., 137

Civic Center, Helena, Mont., 115

Clark, Charles, 93

Clark Fork River, 42, 43

Clark, Senator W. A., 123, 124, 125, 126

Clash, The, 39

*Classic American Ghost Stories,* 138

Cody Hall, Northwest College, Powell, Wyo., 22

Combo, Jerry, 100

Company G, 64

Conan Doyle, Arthur, 80

Conrad Chamber of Commerce, Conrad, Mont., 29

Conrad, Mont., 28, 29

Contemporary Books, 137

Copper King Mansion, Butte, Mont., 123–26, 127, 129

Cote-Smith, Ann, 123–25, 126

*Courier, The,* 70

Crisman Store, Bannack, Mont., 18

Crook, George, 50

Crow Agency, Mont., 50–73

Curran, D. F., 75, 131, 132, 133, 134, 138

Custer Battlefield National Monument, 50–73

Custer, Elizabeth (Libbie), 51, 52

Custer, Lieutenant Colonel George Armstrong, 50, 51, 52, 53, 59, 63, 68, 73

Custer, Thomas, 59


Dacar, Debra, 11, 12, 120

*Daily Ranger,* 6

Dakota Territory, 51

Darelius, Linda, 115

*Dark Trees to the Wind, A Cycle of York State Years,* 27

Daws Street, Lewistown, Mont., 85

DeBoo, Carol, 29

Deer Lodge, Mont., 80, 81, 103

Degelman, Charles F., 86, 87, 88, 89

*Denver Westerners Monthly Roundup, The,* 52

DeWolf, J. M., 71

DiFronzo, Tony, 127

*Dillon Examiner,* 80

Dillon, Mont., 16, 103

*Dillon Tribune,* 15

Dog Creek mountains, 81

Dolson, C. W., 31

Donahue, Michael, 57

Donovan, Roberta, 139

"Door-Stop Skull, The" 138

Downer, Deborah L., 138

Dredger, Jim, 38

Drummond, Mont., 76

Dumas Redlight Antique Mall, Butte, Mont., 4

Dunn, Dorothy, 15, 16, 17

"Durable Tale of Hattie the Hitchhiker, The," 27

Dyer, Dedric Madison, 103–104


Ellingsen, John D., 138

Ellison, Douglas, 62

Elliston, Mont., 10

Elmo, Mont., 28

Ewell, Bert, 85

"Extraordinary Tale of Chief Black Foot, The," 137


Fairchild, Hattie, 27

Farrell Studio, 23

Fine Arts building, University of Montana, Missoula, 33–34

First Avenue North, Billings, Mont., 138

Flathead Lake, 28

Fort Benton, Mont., 5, 28, 29

Fort Laramie, Wyo., 57

Fort Lincoln, 51

Fort Missoula, 3

Frenchwoman, The, 80, 84

Friel (also spelled "Freil"), Mike, 91, 92, 95

Fuller, Chayce (pseudonym), 47, 48

Fuller, Jim (pseudonym), 47, 48, 49

Fuller, Miles, 86, 88, 89, 90, 91, 92, 93, 95, 96, 97, 98, 100, 101

Fuller, Tamara (pseudonym), 47, 48, 49

Fuller, Travis (pseudonym), 47


Gallagher, Fred, 94, 95

Gallahan, Henry, 88

Gardiner, Grace, 120–21
Garnet, Mont., 1, 2, 137, 138
George, Beverly, 126, 128, 129
George, Tom, 126, 128
*Ghosts of the Old West*, 64, 137
"Ghosts on the Little Bighorn," 51
*Ghosts on the Range: Eerie True Tales of Wyoming*, 137
Gibbon, John, 50, 51, 59
Gibson, A. J., 42
Giecek, Rudy, 4
"Girl Named Lavender, The," 26
Glasgow, Mont., 19, 20
Glendive, Mont., 6
Glick, Dr., 16
Goodrich Hotel, Virginia City, Mont., 18
Gordon, Michael, 2, 3
Gordon, Stacey, 5, 34, 46
Gordon, Tim, 46, 134–35
Grand Street Theater, Helena, Mont., 2, 113–22
Grand Street Theater School of Dance, 121
Grasshopper Creek, 15
Graves, Lee, 14–18
Great Falls, Mont., 29, 30
Green, Jerome, 67
Greenough, Edith, 42–46
Greenough, Leo, 45
Greenough Mansion, 42–46
Greenough, Tennie Epperson, 42, 43, 46
Greenough, Thomas, 42, 43, 46
Greenwood Avenue, Butte, Mont., 100
Greyfriar's Bobby, 5
Griffith, Gene, 86, 98–99
Grinnell, George Bird, 138

Haakenson, Vicki, 103–104
Haggins, Aaron, 11, 12, 13, 117, 121
Hangman's Gulch, Bannack, Mont., 14
Hardie, Jean, 119–20
Hardie, Pete, 119
Hardin, Mont., 50, 55, 57, 62
"Heavy Collar and the Ghost Woman," 138
Helena, Mont., 2, 9–13, 14, 25, 26, 28, 29, 80, 81, 102, 113–22
Helena valley, 113
Hennessy department store chain, 126

Hennessy, D. J., 126, 128
Hennessy Mansion, 126, 128–29
Hennessy, Mrs., 129
Highwood Mountains, 138
Hinsdale, Mont., 19
Historical Museum at Fort Missoula, 3
Hoagland, Margaret, 9, 10
Hodgin, Clara Bicknell, 113, 117, 119, 120, 121, 122
Hodgin, Reverend Edwin Stanton, 113
Hodgson, Second Lieutenant Benjamin H., 65, 66
Holmes, Sherlock, 80
Holy, Dave, 45–46
Hope, Christine, 64–66
"Hot Springs Phantom, The," 137
Hugo, Fritz, 90, 93, 95
Humboldt, Iowa, 113
Hunthausen, Bill, 5

*In Memoriam: Clara Bicknell Hodgin*, 113, 117
Interstate 90, 42
"In Touch with the Past: Experiments in Psychometry at Custer Battlefield," 70

Jeannette Rankin Hall, University of Montana, Missoula, 35–37
"Joe," 55, 56
Johnson, Daniel, 43
Johnson, Dorothy, 19, 20, 21, 22
Johnson, Keith, 22
Johnson, Linda, 19, 21, 22
Jones, Louis C., 27, 28
Jordan, Robert Paul, 51, 52
Judd, Patrick, 126, 128, 129
Judith Gap Mercantile, 138
Judith Gap, Mont., 138
Julie, 12

Kalanick, A. J., 29, 30, 107–12
Kalanick, Hilda, 30
Keller, Doug, 62, 63, 66, 72
Kelly, Marty, 138
Kelly, Matthew (pseudonym), 9, 10, 11
"Ken," 125–26
King, Evelyn, 3
King, Stephen, 87
Knights Templar, 133

Kowalczyk, Ken, 138
Kowalczyk, Patti, 138
Kraul, Edward Garcia, 137
Kuhlman, Charles, 52

"La Llorona, the Weeping Woman," 137
Lane, George, 116
Last Stand Hill, Little Bighorn Battle-
field National Monument, 52, 53, 67,
73
Las Vegas, N.Mex., 137
"Laurie (Strange Things Happen)," 32
"Lavender," 27
Leaf, Jim, 6
Lee, Dickie, 32
Legendary Lodge, 5
*Legend into History,* 52
*Legend of La Llorona, The,* 137
*Legend of the House in White Sulphur: A
Bit of Montana Folklore, The,* 138–39
Leisure Highlands Golf Course, 42
Leonard, Guy, 55, 61
Leonard, Janet, 61
Lewis and Clark Library, Helena,
Mont., 113
Lewistown, Mont., 85
Lincoln, Nebr., 138
Lippert, Sadie, 30–31
"Little Bighorn, The," 64
Little Bighorn Associates, 66
Little Bighorn Battlefield National
Monument, 2, 50–73, 137
Little Bighorn River, 50, 64, 65
Little Bighorn Valley, 70
Little Bitterroot, 28
Loos, Karen, 120
Luce, Evelyn, 54
Luce, Major Edward S., 53, 59

Madison Street, Missoula, Mont., 43
Main Hall, University of Montana, Mis-
soula, 37–39
Maloughney, Pat, 100
Malta, Mont., 19
Malyevac, Larry, 100, 101
Mangum, Neil, 63, 72
Mansion Restaurant, Missoula, Mont.,
42–46
Martinez, Dan, 60, 73
Martin, Paul, 115

"Mary," 5
Massie, Mike, 57
Massie, Ruth, 57
Mathews, Bertie, 15, 16, 17
Mathews, Georgia, 16
Mattfeldt, Duane, 19, 20
Mattfeldt, Mary Johnson, 19–24
Mauricio, the Reverend Victoria, 137
McCarthy, Dan J., 95–96
McCormick, Andrea, 123
McDonald, Archie, 105–106
McDonald, Malcolm, 104–106
McDonald Pass, 25, 26
McDonald, Tommy, 105
McLaughlin, Don, 116
McLaughlin, Janet, 117–18
Meade Hotel, Bannack, Mont., 15, 16,
17
Medicine Tail Coulee, Little Bighorn
Battlefield National Monument, 73
Medicine Tail Ford, Little Bighorn
Battlefield National Monument, 69
Meeks, Lorrie McDonald, 28, 104–106
Meeteetse, Wyo., 137
Meinholtz, Rolly, 35
Miles City, Mont., 47–49
Miller, David, 9, 25, 26, 28, 29
Minneapolis, Minn., 66
Missoula County Courthouse, 42
Missoula, Mont., 3, 25, 33–39, 42–46,
76, 77, 138
*Missoulian,* 3
Mondloch, Jack, 35–36, 38
Montana College of Mineral Science
and Technology, 126
Montana Department of Fish, Wildlife
and Parks, 18
Montana Historical Society, 14
*Montana Magazine,* 28, 31
Montana Repertory Theater, 33
*Montana Standard,* 4, 86, 98, 99, 100,
123, 124, 130
Montana State University, Bozeman, 19,
111, 139
Montana Street, Butte, Mont., 100
Montana Territory, 14
Montana 28, 28
Moore, Michael, 56, 57–59
Morrow, Mary Vollmer, 33–34, 115,
118, 119

Mosby, A. J., 42, 43, 45, 46
Mosby, Ruth Greenough, 42, 46
Mount Mariah Cemetery, Butte, Mont., 100–101
Mulcahy, Deputy Sheriff Tom, 89, 90–94, 95
Mulhair, Charles, 54, 63, 64
Mulhair, Karol, 54, 63, 64
Munn, Debra D., 137
Murray, Earl, 64, 65, 137
"Mysteries of Old Garnet," 137
Mysteries of the Unknown, 5
"Mystery of the Little People, The," 137
Mystery Stalks the Prairie, 139

National Cemetery, Little Bighorn Battlefield National Monument, 52, 56, 61, 64, 66
National Enquirer, 68
National Geographic, 51, 68
National Park Service, 67, 70
Neitz, Trilby, 78
Nelson, Cliff, 67
New Orleans, La., 66
New York, 26, 27
Niarada, Mont., 28, 104, 105
Nixon, Diane, 101
Noonan, Ed, 11, 12, 117
Norfolk, Va., 137
Northwest College, Powell, Wyo., 22
Nye-Cartwright Ridge, 69

O'Connell, Kathryn, 11, 102–103, 119, 120
O'Hara, Violet, 138
Old Nick, 32
"Old One-Eye and Other Lost Souls," 31
Olson, Kathi, 3
O'Rourke, Sheriff, 89, 95

Page, Dolly, 78
Pan American Publishing Company, 137
Park Street, Butte, Mont., 129
Penrod, Jackie, 118
Penrod, Rick, 118
Petersen family, 74–79
Petersen, Frances (pseudonym), 74, 75, 76, 78

Petersen, James (pseudonym), 74, 75, 76, 77
Petersen, Judith (pseudonym), 74, 75, 76, 77
Petersen, Paul (pseudonym), 74, 75, 76
Phantom Encounters, 5
Philipsburg, Mont., 74–79, 138
Plainfeather, Mardell, 56–57, 67–69
Plummer, Henry, 14, 16, 18
Plummer, Maggie, 28
Poe, Cora, 115
Poole, Dan, 121
Poole, Sidney, 121
Popular Science, 27
Pross, Beth, 2

Quinn, J. J., 89

Ramapo River, N.Y., 26
Ranger-Review, 6
Rattlesnake Creek, 42
Raynesford, 139
Reader's Digest, 26
Reader's Guide to Periodical Literature, The, 26
Reardon family (pseudonym), 132–34
Reardon, Mr., 132, 133–34
Reardon, Mrs., 132, 133–34
Reece, Bob, 52, 59, 60, 62, 66, 69
Reinhardt, Tana, 6
Reno, Major Marcus, 50, 51, 63, 64, 65, 71
Reno Retreat Crossing, Little Bighorn Battlefield National Monument, 64, 65, 66, 71
Return of Chief Black Foot, The, 137
Richards, L. Jane, 3
Rickey, Dr. Don, 69–70
Road Agents, 14, 16, 18
Rock of Gibraltar, 123
Rock, Roger, 4
Rodgers, Joni, 115–16, 117–18
Rolling Stones, 33, 39
Ruzevich, Pete, 10

St. Albert's Hall, Carroll College, Helena, Mont., 11
St. Charles Hall, Carroll College, Helena, Mont., 9, 10, 11, 12
St. Louis, Mo., 75

Salmon Lake, 5
Santa Fe, N.Mex., 137
Schneider, Jerry, 115
Seventh Cavalry, 50, 51, 53, 66
Shelby clan, 138
"Shep," 5
Sheridan, Paula, 44–45
"Simone," 2
Sitting Bull, 52
Skinner's Saloon, Bannack, Mont., 14
Soto, Rick, 97–98, 99, 100
Soubier, Cliff, 67
Spokane, Wash., 42
"Spooky Niarada: Where things go
    'bump' in the night," 28
Starkel, Howard R., 69–72
Stockham, Clancy, 125
Stoke-on-Trent, England, 53
Stone House, Little Bighorn Battlefield
    National Monument, 56–61, 62
Student Union, Carroll College, Helena,
    Mont., 11
Summit, Chris, 63

Tallmadge, Jeanne, 35–36
Tash, Dr. Dale, 16
Tebbetts, Lieutenant Clinton H., 66
Terry, Alfred, 50, 51, 59
Tiffany, Louis Comfort, 113
Tongue River, 48
True Hauntings in Montana, 75, 131, 138
True West, 138

Unitarian church, Helena, Mont., 113,
    115, 116
University Hall, University of Mon-
    tana, Missoula, 37–39
University of Montana, Missoula,
    33–39, 138
Utley, Robert, 52

"Valerie," 23
Valier, Mont., 28, 29
Van Buren Street bridge, Missoula,
    Mont., 42
Vancouver, Wash., 103, 104
Vial, John, 81
Vigilantes, 14
Virginia City, Mont., 2, 18, 103
"Visions of Reno Crossing," 64, 137
Visitor center, Little Bighorn Battlefield
    National Monument, 52–56, 65
"Visitors of Another Kind," 52
Voice of the Prairie, 120
Volunteer in the Parks program, 61,
    62

Wagner, Maria, 123
Ward, Andrew, 64
Waring, Stephen, 53, 54
Weeping Woman: Encounters with La
    Llorona, The, 137
Western Montana College, Dillon,
    16
West, MaryJane, 39
West Yellowstone, 107
Whitehall, Mont., 40–41
White Sulphur Springs, Mont., 139
Whitford, C. S., Dr., 80, 81–84
Williams, Bob, 36–38
Wilson, Darla Bruner, 3
Wing, Steve, 34
Wolverton, Keith, 139
Woodthorpe, Henry, 95, 96

Xavier Renois House, Bannack, Mont.,
    18

Yellowstone River, 48, 137
Yonce, Fritzie, 45, 46